MARKIEVICZ
A Most Outrageous Rebel

LINDIE NAUGHTON

MERRION
PRESS

First published in 2016 by
Merrion Press
10 George's Street
Newbridge
Co. Kildare
Ireland
www.merrionpress.ie

British Library Cataloguing in Publication Data
An entry can be found on request

ISBN: 978-1-78537-221-6 (Paper)
ISBN: 978-1-78537-084-7 (Kindle)

Library of Congress Cataloging in Publication Data
An entry can be found on request

Design by www.jminfotechindia.com
Typeset in Minion Pro 11.5/14 pt
Cover design by www.phoenix-graphicdesign.com
Front cover image: Seated studio portrait of Constance Markievicz,
c.1915. (Image Courtesy of the National Library of Ireland & NLI Logo)
Back cover image: Lissadell House, Co. Sligo. Photo by the author

3. Portrait of Constance Markievicz from about 1908. (Reproduced courtesy of the National Library of Ireland)

4. Constance Markievicz with a group of Fianna boys (undated). (Reproduced courtesy of the National Library of Ireland)

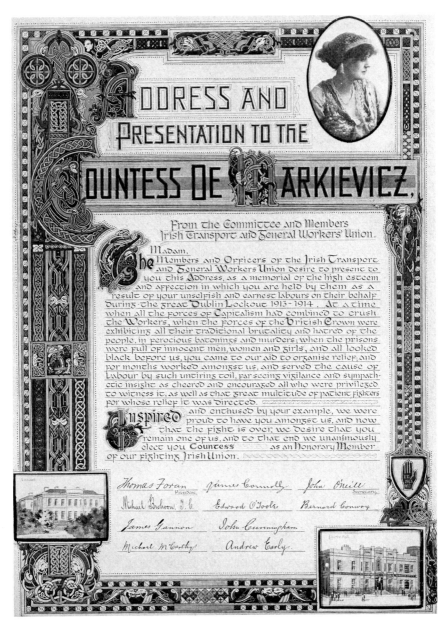

ADDRESS AND PRESENTATION TO THE COUNTESS DE MARKIEVICZ,

From the Committee and Members
Irish Transport and General Workers' Union.

Madam,

The Members and Officers of the Irish Transport and General Workers Union desire to present to you this Address, as a memorial of the high esteem and affection in which you are held by them as a result of your unselfish and earnest labours on their behalf during the great Dublin Lockout 1913-1914. At a time when all the forces of Capitalism had combined to crush the Workers, when the forces of the British Crown were exhibiting all their traditional brutality and hatred of the people, in ferocious batonings and murders; when the prisons were full of innocent men, women and girls, and all looked black before us, you came to our aid to organise relief, and for months worked amongst us, and served the cause of Labour by such untiring toil, far seeing vigilance and sympathetic insight as cheered and encouraged all who were privileged to witness it, as well as that great multitude of patient fighters for whose relief it was directed.

Inspired and enthused by your example, we were proud to have you amongst us, and now that the fight is over, we desire that you remain one of us, and to that end we unanimously elect you Countess as an Honorary Member of our fighting Irish Union.

Thomas Foran
President

James Connolly

John O'Neill
Secretary

Michael Brohoon, T.C.

Edward O'Toole

Bernard Conway

James Gannon

John Cunningham

Michael McCarthy

Andrew Early.

5. Address presented to Constance Markievicz by the Irish Transport and General Workers' Union for her work during the 1913 lock-out. (Reproduced courtesy of the National Library of Ireland)

6. Constance Markievicz as Joan of Arc appearing to a woman political prisoner played by Kathleen Houston in a *tableau vivant*, 1914. (Reproduced courtesy of the National Library of Ireland)

7. Seated studio portrait of Constance Markievicz, around 1915. (Reproduced courtesy of the National Library of Ireland)

8. Surrey House on Leinster Road in Rathmines, Dublin (on left), where Constance Markievicz was living in 1916. Next door is Dorset House. (Photograph by the author)

9. Constance Markievicz in military uniform, around 1915. (Reproduced courtesy of the National Library of Ireland)

10. Royal Fusiliers' Arch (also known as Traitors' Arch), St Stephen's Green, Dublin, through which the Irish Citizen Army marched on Easter Monday 1916. (Photograph by the author)

11. The Royal College of Surgeons in Ireland on St Stephen's Green, Dublin. Note the bullets marks on the facade. (Photograph by the author)

12. Poem by Dora Sigerson Shorter which was illustrated by Constance Markievicz while in Aylesbury Prison in 1917 and given to Gerard Crofts as a belated wedding gift. (Reproduced courtesy of the National Library of Ireland)

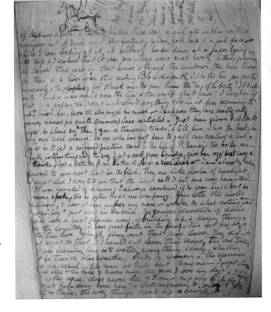

13. One of Constance Markievicz's letters to her sister Eva from Aylesbury Prison, dated 14 May 1917, saved by Esther Roper. (Reproduced courtesy of the National Library of Ireland from MS5673)

14. Watercolour of a horse leaping over the prison walls from one of Constance Markievicz's letters from Aylesbury Prison in the spring of 1917. (Reproduced courtesy of the National Library of Ireland from MS5673)

15. Peace meeting at Mansion House, Dublin, 1921. Left to right: Kathleen Clarke, Constance Markievicz, Kate O'Callaghan and Margaret Pearse. (Reproduced courtesy of the National Library of Ireland)

16. Éamon de Valera and Constance Markievicz standing in a garden (undated). (Reproduced courtesy of the National Library of Ireland)

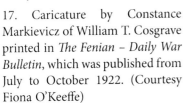

17. Caricature by Constance Markievicz of William T. Cosgrave printed in *The Fenian – Daily War Bulletin*, which was published from July to October 1922. (Courtesy Fiona O'Keeffe)

18. Statue of Constance Markievicz by Seamus Murphy (1954) in St Stephen's Green, Dublin. (Photograph by the author)

sent to Belfast; she returned with Lillie Connolly. The Connolly family was to stay at Constance's cottage during the Rising. With them they brought all their possessions, leaving for ever their home of five years.

Bad luck and the IRB's addiction to secrecy bedevilled preparations for the Rising in the final few days. Although MacNeill was technically head of the Volunteers, he had not been told the date of the Rising by the Military Council. Bulmer Hobson, still a member of the IRB, was likewise unaware of plans. Wild stories were circulating in the provinces and, on Thursday, Commandant Liam Manahan arrived from Limerick at the Volunteers' headquarters in Dawson Street seeking information. The contents of the 'Castle document' had made him and many other Volunteer commandants uneasily aware that they had little information to go on. Bulmer Hobson, who knew no better, assured him that nothing exceptional was planned.

Later that evening, Hobson and J.J. O'Connell, a Volunteer officer, overheard enough of a conversation to make them suspect that a rising was indeed planned for the Sunday. They immediately set off for MacNeill's house, where they reported the conversation. The three then headed for St Enda's to confront Patrick Pearse. It was after midnight when they arrived. When Pearse confirmed their assumptions, MacNeill was furious both about the secrecy surrounding the plans and what he saw as the folly of calling out a poorly prepared army at a strategically bad time. He warned Pearse that he would do everything he could to stop the Rising, short of informing the Castle. Supported by The O'Rahilly, MacNeill's first step was to send out an order cancelling 'all orders issued by Commandant Pearse or by any other person heretofore'.

Pearse summoned Seán Mac Diarmada and Thomas MacDonagh for an urgent meeting and, early on Friday morning, the trio arrived at MacNeill's house. They told him that Roger Casement was bringing a shipload of arms from Germany and that the Rising must begin on Easter Sunday. The arrival of arms removed one of MacNeill's objections. He accepted that the Rising was inevitable and sent out a second round of dispatches, this time confirming that the announced manoeuvres would take place as originally planned. The result was utter confusion, not helped when the German arms failed to arrive. One Munster commandant remembered getting five separate orders.

On Thursday, off the coast of Kerry, the *Aud*, a German ship disguised as a Norwegian trawler, lay off Fenit pier waiting for a signal from the shore. In a disastrous failure of communication, the local Volunteer officer did not expect the boat until the weekend. Indeed, the entire adventure was doomed to failure when the schedule was changed after a submarine along with the *Aud* had set sail from the German naval base of Heligoland. On board the submarine were Roger Casement, Robert Monteith and a member of the Irish Brigade called Sergeant Beverly (under the name 'Daniel Bailey'). Unknown to them, the British Secret Service had cracked German radio codes and, for some time, had known of Casement's machinations and of the planned Rising. They had asked Augustine Birrell to arrest the prominent Sinn Féin leaders but, since they could not tell him why, he was not convinced.

While Pearse and MacNeill were meeting in Dublin in the early hours of Friday morning, Robert Monteith, with Casement and 'Daniel Bailey', had gone ashore to supervise the landing of arms and ammunition from the *Aud*. A local farmer walking along Banna Strand noticed the three strangers and alerted the Royal Irish Constabulary. 'Bailey' was arrested along with Austin Stack and Con Collins, who were the local contacts.

A second attempt to collect the shipment also failed. Five men had left Dublin for Killarney by train on Friday morning. They drove away in two cars and, in the pitch black night, one of the cars took a wrong turning and drove off a pier at Ballykissane. Three of the men drowned. The other car waited for three hours past rendezvous time and, when no one showed up, returned to Dublin. At sea, the *Aud* was seized by the watching British naval forces and brought to Cork.

Monteith was still at large and his main concern was to get a message to MacNeill that the arms had not arrived and that it might be wise to call off the planned insurrection. The message was delivered not to MacNeill or Bulmer Hobson as Monteith had ordered but to James Connolly at Liberty Hall. Connolly called an emergency meeting with Pearse and others and gave them Monteith's message. After much discussion, the Military Council decided to go ahead with the Rising. Pearse and Mac Diarmada saw MacNeill on Saturday morning and told him of Casement's arrest.

In Cork, the *Aud* and her British escort had arrived in Queenstown harbour. Lifeboats were lowered and the crew members in their German uniforms jumped in. No sooner were they safe than the ship exploded, with 20,000 rifles, ten machine guns and one million rounds of ammunition lost. The news quickly arrived in Dublin and decided MacNeill's next move. On Saturday afternoon, he met a number of activists including Arthur Griffith, Joseph Plunkett and Thomas MacDonagh; he told them that he planned to cancel all orders for Sunday.

Plunkett and MacDonagh, both members of the Military Council, objected strenuously, but MacNeill was adamant that it was his duty to save the Volunteers from useless slaughter. Among the messengers who set out for the provinces was The O'Rahilly, who left his all-too recognisable De Dion Bouton car at home and took a taxi to deliver cancellation orders in six counties before ending up in Limerick the following morning. Late on Monday, news would reach him of the Rising. He was driven back to Dublin and joined in the fighting. His reason was simple: 'Well, I've helped to wind up the clock – I might as well hear it strike!' To Constance he commented, 'It is madness, but it is glorious madness.' He fought in the GPO and would die during the retreat.

On Saturday evening, Eoin MacNeill made a mad dash by bicycle to the offices of the *Sunday Independent* with a copy of the order rescinding Sunday manoeuvres. He arrived just in time to make the morning paper.

Those in Liberty Hall were continuing with their plans. The women cooked hams and sliced bread to make hundreds of sandwiches for the 'ration packs'. William O'Brien, Winifred Carney and Constance prepared mobilisation orders and officers' commissions. Constance's own commission as a lieutenant was typed out by Winifred Carney and signed by Connolly. A friend came to the hall and, noticing the general bustle, assumed the Liberty Players were getting ready for a production. 'Rehearsing I suppose?' she said to Constance.

'Yes,' replied Constance.
'Is it for children?' asked her friend.
'No,' said Constance; 'for grown-ups.'

The mobilisation orders for the Citizen Army were sent out: they were to meet at Liberty Hall at 3.30pm on Sunday, with full equipment. With most of the Citizen Army living in Dublin, assembling them was relatively easy. Meanwhile, Volunteer messengers were spreading out around the country by train, tram and bicycle since cars were rare in those days. The messages had to be delivered in secrecy to someone known. It took time, and those who felt the Volunteers were not ready to fight had some reason on their side.

Others believed in the words of Fintan Lalor to Young Ireland before the 1848 Rebellion: 'Somewhere and somehow and by someone, a beginning must be made, and the first act of armed resistance is always premature, imprudent and foolish.'

CHAPTER ELEVEN

Easter Week 1916 –
Year One of Irish History

Sunday newspapers in Ireland traditionally made most of their sales outside churches, with posters on railings proclaiming the big stories of the day.

On Sunday, 23 April 1916, the men, women and children attending Easter services could not fail to notice the placards announcing that Volunteer manoeuvres planned for later in the day had been cancelled. The headlines took up much of the space on the front page of the *Sunday Independent*, and for those who knew what was afoot, this was devastating news. Few associated the move with two other items on the page: one concerned the seizure of arms in County Kerry and the other a tragic accident, also in Kerry, in which three men drowned after their car took a wrong turning. The day was to pass in 'doubts, grumblings and rumours', as one Volunteer put it.

When Constance saw the front page, she raced to Liberty Hall 'heart-broken' and found James Connolly and Seán Mac Diarmada sitting with Tom Clarke at a table in the small bedroom Connolly used at the back of the building. She believed that 'Professor Eoin MacNeill and Mr B. Hobson had treacherously acted a coward's part, secretly through the Irish Republican Brotherhood (IRB), and publicly through the daily papers'. She got that wrong – Hobson had been placed under house arrest by the IRB Military Council, fearing his influence over MacNeill.

Markievicz, as well as Clarke and Connolly, knew that MacNeill's action had ended what little chance the rebels had of holding out long enough to influence public opinion and save the lives of the leaders. That MacNeill's move was intended to save lives meant nothing. 'There is only one sort of responsibility I am afraid of and that is preventing the men and women of Ireland fighting and dying for Ireland if they are so minded' was how Connolly put it.

The day that followed was the 'busiest I have ever lived through', wrote Constance later. 'Messengers came and went, and the Provisional Government of the Republic sat the whole day in Connolly's little room.' By one o'clock, it was settled. Although MacNeill had 'cut the ground from under their feet', they would carry on as planned, although a day later, knowing that the decision would mean certain death for the leaders. Despite the knowledge that, after years of meticulous preparation, much would be left to chance, the mood was one of euphoria: 'the cloud had passed' said Constance.

After Dublin Castle heard that Roger Casement was in custody, orders were prepared to arrest other rebel leaders. These had to be signed, but with senior officials away for the holiday weekend, this was not possible. When under-secretary Matthew Nathan and army officers read the notice in the newspapers cancelling 'manoeuvres', they relaxed their guard.

Since the Citizen Army had been mobilised for the Sunday, the planned drill went ahead to give the impression that all was normal. Shortly after 4pm, the men were on their usual march with Connolly and his second-in-command Michael Mallin at the head; Constance marched not far behind. From Liberty Hall they made their way to St Stephen's Green, then on to Dublin Castle, where they were observed by the guard on duty, before returning to Liberty Hall via the quays. In Beresford Place, Connolly made what would be his final public speech. Referring to the question of England brokering a peace deal with Germany, he said that, at such negotiations, Ireland should be represented. 'You are now under arms. You will not lay down your arms until your have struck a blow for Ireland!' he said in conclusion. The men cheered and shots were fired into the air; the watching police made no move.

During the day, the Proclamation of the Irish Republic was printed in Liberty Hall by a group including the trade unionist Rosie Hackett; she remembered the men resenting the presence of women in the room. After the 'Proclamation' rolled off the press, one story has Constance picking up a copy and reading it out to a small crowd that had assembled in Beresford Place. All the signatories to the Proclamation were men but, if this story is true, it was Constance, a woman, who was first to read the Proclamation in public. All but one of the seven signatories had agreed to its theme of equal rights for men and women, and Hanna Sheehy Skeffington had been chosen as a member of a civil provisional government should the Rising succeed.

To explain the large numbers congregating around Liberty Hall, the usual Sunday night concert went ahead. Nerves were on edge: 'The day dragged through somehow, the night passed with little rest for anyone, and next morning we were all at our posts at cockcrow, everybody in the highest spirits.'

Along with Winifred Carney, who was Connolly's secretary, Constance was spending the night at the William O'Brien household in Belvedere Place. After the family had gone to bed, they heard a shot. While unloading her automatic, an exhausted Constance had fired a shot through the door of the O'Brien's bedroom. Fortunately, no one was hurt. The next morning, she arose and put on the uniform that Nora Connolly had already seen – the tunic that had belonged to Seamus Mallin, which fitted her well although the sleeves were short, along with jodhpurs, boots and her favourite hat with its plume of feathers. She and Margaret Skinnider were the only women to wear military uniform that week.

At 10am on Easter Monday, the four city Volunteer battalions were to parade with full arms and equipment, each commandant announcing the plans for his men. Every man was armed with a rifle and a pike. From Larkfield in Kimmage came fifty-six men from England and Scotland, who travelled into town by tram.

Constance remembered seeing Tom Clarke in those last few moments.

> Happy proud and gay was Tom Clarke on that day. His life's work had borne fruit at last ... we met for a few minutes just before the time fixed to march out. It seems queer, looking back on it, how no-one spoke of death or fear or defeat. I remember saying goodbye to Tom Clarke just at the door of Dr Kathleen Lynn's little surgery ... We then went downstairs, and each man joined up with his little band.

Pearse, provisional president of the Irish Republic, was there with a group of Irish Volunteers from St Enda's; so too was Thomas MacDonagh. Connolly, as Commandant-General of all the insurgent forces in Dublin, told the troops that there was no longer a Citizen Army and a Volunteer force but an Irish Republican Army that included the female members of the Citizen Army ambulance corps. He made it clear that they were to fire their guns only as a last resort, for defensive purposes. No one counted the little band; it numbered about a thousand, far short of the 5,000 originally expected. When William O'Brien asked Connolly whether there was any chance of success, he replied 'None whatever'.

At 11.45am, bugler William Oman sounded the fall-in and Connolly and his men set off along Abbey Street towards Sackville Street and the GPO. It was a motley army; some were in full uniform, others in hats, leggings and militaristic tunics. Many wore only armbands. 'Each man had a different kind of kit. No two had it affixed in the same way and probably no-one could have put it on in the same way twice,' remembered John Gallogly. A group of men pulled two drays loaded with pistols, shot guns, rifles, explosives and home-made bombs assembled with tin cans and gelignite.

At the end of Abbey Street, Connolly gave the order: 'Right turn – the GPO. Charge!' In Kathleen Clarke's account, Tom Clarke, as president and first signatory of the Proclamation, was the man to lead the rebels into the GPO, followed by Mac Diarmada, Plunkett, Connolly and Pearse. Clarke and Mac Diarmada, one elderly, the other lame, had driven to Sackville Street. In the GPO, a few customers buying stamps were bustled out of the building. A Royal Fusiliers lieutenant who was sending a telegram was taken prisoner, along with the sentries guarding the telegram room. Those still at Liberty Hall could hear the distant sound of breaking glass as windows were smashed to clear the line of fire. Within minutes, both the tricolour and Constance's home-made flag were fluttering above the building. The rebels in the street below raised a cheer.

It was now Constance's turn.

> I stood on the steps and watched the little bodies of men and
> women march off, Pearse and Connolly to the GPO, Seán Connolly

to the City Hall, all marching proudly, confident that they were doing right, sure at last that they had made the subjection of Ireland impossible for generations to come. I went off then with the Doctor [Lynn] in her car. We carried a large store of First Aid necessities and drove off through quiet dusty streets and across the river, reaching the City Hall just at the very moment that Commandant Seán Connolly and his little troop of men and women swung around the corner and he raised his gun and shot the policeman who barred the way. A wild excitement ensued, people running from every side to see what was up. The Doctor got out, and I remember Mrs Barrett and others helping to carry in the Doctor's bundles.

Constable James O'Brien from Kilfergus, County Limerick – unarmed – had fallen victim to the first shot of the Rebellion; an ugly start. In the delirium that followed, the rebels did not appear to realise that the half-empty Castle was theirs for the taking; only six soldiers were on guard that day, backed up by a garrison of less than twenty-five in the Ship Street Barracks beside it. At the GPO, Patrick Pearse had stepped out of the building and read the Proclamation of the new Irish Republic, claiming 'the allegiance of every Irishman and Irishwoman', to a handful of bemused Dubliners.

After Constance had left Beresford Place, it was the turn of Captain Richard McCormick and his group, who marched up Eden Quay making for Harcourt Street Station. The St Stephen's Green group moved off soon after. The original plan for the south side of the city was to capture the Green and surrounding buildings and make it the base for an army of 5,000 rebels after the nearby barracks were captured. Surrounding the twenty acres of the Green were at least two hotels and numerous private clubs and houses, where soldiers and prisoners could be billeted. On the east side was St Vincent's Hospital, with the Meath and Adelaide hospitals also close by; the wounded would be well looked after. Inside was a lake that would guarantee a water supply.

The outpost at nearby Jacob's would control access to Dublin Castle from Portobello Barracks, as would the two small outposts at Davy's pub on Portobello Bridge and at Harcourt Street station. Bolands

Mills on Ringsend Road would control the roads from the ferry at Kingstown, about ten miles from the GPO; to stop trains arriving from Dublin's southern suburbs, the garrison quickly ripped up a section of the railway line.

The actress and Cumann na mBan member Máire Nic Shiublaigh, had cycled to her post at Jacob's biscuit factory. After she arrived, she looked out of a window on the Peter Street side of the building and saw an open two-seater car swaying from side to side. As it drew alongside Jacob's, a figure in Citizen Army uniform stood up in the front seat and waved a hat. With Kathleen Lynn remaining at City Hall, Constance was on her way to St Stephen's Green with the rest of the first aid supplies. 'Go at it boys!' she yelled. 'The Citizen Army are taking the Green! Dublin Castle is falling!' Dublin Castle never fell; the Green held out for only a day.

Dr Lynn's car was one of the few available to the insurgents and was manned by a Volunteer called Mark Cummins, who was described by Lynn as 'a most reckless driver'. His job was to transport Constance between the rebel posts, but the car ended up as part of a barricade on St Stephen's Green and it was months before Dr Lynn saw it again. For the rebels, the bicycle would prove a far more effective means of moving around the city.

When they arrived at the top of Grafton Street, the main body of rebels marched through the Dublin Fusiliers' Arch into the Green. Thomas O'Donoghue and his group wheeled left, marched to the Shelbourne Hotel corner and entered the Green through the gate there.

Constance arrived at St Stephen's Green between one o'clock and two o'clock, according to the pageboy at the University Club at her trial following the Rising. By the time she arrived, the Green was occupied by a hundred Irish Citizen Army soldiers. When the Irish Citizen Army troops arrived, they had seen Thomas MacDonagh's troops parading on the west side of the Green in front of the Royal College of Surgeons before marching off towards Cuffe Street to take over the Jacob's building. MacDonagh's second-in-command was Maud Gonne's ex-husband, John MacBride, who had come to Dublin to meet his brother and could not resist joining the fight. It would cost him his life.

Margaret Skinnider, sent off as an advance scout by Mallin, had arrived at the Green on her bicycle. There were no soldiers in sight; all she could see was a single unarmed policeman, who paid no attention to her. He was probably Constable Michael Lahiff who, at around noon, was shot, allegedly by Constance. After he fell, Constance had run triumphantly into the Green crying 'I got him' according to an account, typewritten a year after the event, by Geraldene [sic] Fitzgerald, a nurse at the St Patrick's Nursing Home on the south-west corner of St Stephen's Green. Yet when Lahiff was shot, within five minutes of the Green's occupation, Constance was still on her way from City Hall, as witnessed by Máire Nic Shiublaigh. At her court martial, no mention is made of her killing an unarmed policeman, or indeed of killing anyone. Later, Father Sherwin of the Catholic University church on St Stephen's Green wrote to Josslyn to assure him that 'it was not your sister who fired the shot. She has given me leave to state that this is a fact.'

Several months later, Constance told Eva that she had held a revolver at a policeman's chest but could not pull the trigger to shoot him because she realised that she knew him. She admitted that she shot another in the arm 'as he jumped'. Lahiff was sent to the Meath Hospital and died half an hour after he was admitted. The death certificate described the cause as 'a bullet through both lungs and left arm'. If she had shot him, Constance may not have been aware that he later died.

Was there anyone else who could have shot Constable Lahiff? The available facts are that he was at St Stephen's Green, that he was unarmed and that he was shot at around noon. When Margaret Skinnider arrived at the south side of the Green, she reported that she saw only a single policeman in the area that day. A few minutes later, when the Irish Citizen Army arrived, James O'Shea remarked in his witness statement that a policeman passed a comment about them playing at soldiers. He decided to get his revenge. 'We had orders not to fire until we heard firing from Harcourt Street, so when firing was on for a minute or two, I went to the gate to fire at the policeman, who had passed the remarks earlier. He was at Noblett's Corner at the time so I had a shot at him.' What is not recorded is whether O'Shea's shot hit or even killed the policeman.

Noblett's Corner was at the junction of Grafton Street and South King Street, facing St Stephen's Green; O'Shea's immediate orders were to dig trenches inside the Dawson Street entrance to the Green. While digging the trench, a man stumbled up, pretending to be drunk. O'Shea decided he was a spy and, by his own account, shot him dead at close quarters. Although Connolly had given orders to members of the Irish Citizen Army that no unarmed soldier or policeman was to be shot, the police were held in contempt by many Dubliners because of their behaviour during the 1913 lock-out. Certainly O'Shea had no qualms about killing a perceived enemy. Three unarmed Dublin policemen were killed in the opening hours of the Rising, which caused them to be withdrawn from the streets, to the serious detriment of public order.

After Commandant Mallin arrived at St Stephen's Green and seized the keys to the park, he had ordered his men to start digging deep trenches beside the hedges just inside the railings. Others were ordered to make barricades on the roads ringing the Green and commandeered a large laundry van, a side car, a dray and two private cars. These battle techniques had worked well in countries, such as India, where Mallin had served during his British army days. Whether they were suitable for the wide streets of a Georgian city like Dublin is open to argument. No effort was made to seize the buildings around the Green. With fewer men than he had hoped, Mallin had asked Constance to remain with his group, leaving her in charge of the trenches and barricades and then nominating her as his second-in-command. Guests staying in the Shelbourne Hotel, many of them in Dublin for the Fairyhouse races, gathered at the windows to observe the strange goings-on. They caught little more than the occasional glint of a rifle or a glimpse of a uniformed figure among the bushes.

They had something to talk about when Constance, with a rifle on her shoulder, began marching up and down in front of the hotel. A woman in uniform was an unusual sight, to say the least. When some British officers in the Shelbourne Hotel and the United Services Club began shooting at the Green, Constance quietened them by returning their fire. She wrote later: 'This work was very exciting when the fighting began. I continued round and round the Green, reporting back if anything was wanted, or tackling any sniper who was particularly objectionable.'

Later that day, the writer James Stephens, puzzled by groups of people standing near his office on Merrion Row, asked a 'kindly-looking lad' armed with a gun what was going on. He was told that the city had been 'taken' by republican rebels and that they held the GPO and had seized Dublin Castle. Many of the rebels were teenagers; the youngest was twelve-year-old Tommy Keenan, who fought alongside Constance at the Royal College of Surgeons, hiding his Fianna shirt under a jumper when he left the building with messages or to find food. Because he was so small, no one paid him any attention.

The curious crowd that had gathered at Merrion Row, which leads on to the Green, was initially unconcerned about the danger they put themselves in. All that changed when an elderly man, who had been warned several times not to remove his lorry from a barricade, was shot dead by a young rebel near the Shelbourne Hotel. At the sound of the gunfire, women began crying and shrieking and falling to their knees.

As soon as the small troop was established in the Green, Margaret Skinnider cycled down Leeson Street towards the Grand Canal to see if there was any sign of British soldiers leaving Beggar's Bush or Portobello Barracks. Everything remained quiet. She was then sent to the Harcourt Street train station, where she found that Captain McCormick and his men had managed to cut the telegraph and telephone wires, a priority for all the battalions at their posts. Because one telephone wire was missed, word of the Rising reached London sooner than expected.

Back at the Green, the men were busy digging themselves in, using shrubbery as protection. Two British officers were taken prisoner. Afterwards, they complimented the rebels on how well they had been treated. According to Skinnider, soldiers from Portobello Barracks were sent out twice on Monday to clear the Green. The first time they were stopped at Portobello bridge when they were fired on by three snipers from the roof of Davy's pub. They backed off, not realising that the pub was held by only eight men. Then, at dusk, Skinnider was on her way back from the GPO when she saw two people hurrying from the Green. They were William Partridge and Constance. At the same time, she saw British soldiers advancing up Harcourt Street.

> The countess stood motionless waiting for them to come near ... At length she raised her gun to her shoulder – it was an 'automatic' over a foot long, which she had converted into a short rifle by taking out the wooden holster and using it as a stock – and took aim. Neither she nor Partridge noticed me as I came up behind

them. I was quite close when they fired. The shots rang out at the same moment and I saw the two officers leading the column drop to the street. As the countess was taking aim again, the soldiers, without firing a shot, turned and ran in great confusion for their barracks. The whole company fled as fast as they could from two people, one of them a woman!

This episode may have been what the nurse Geraldene Fitzgerald witnessed.

The plans to establish outposts that would give the rebels in the Green time to dig themselves in before troops arrived from Portobello Barracks did not work out. When Sergeant Joe Doyle and his seven men realised that they were facing 650 men led by twenty-one officers of the 3rd Irish Rifles who were assembling at Portobello Barracks, they swiftly retreated from their post in Davy's pub.

Lack of manpower meant that moves to secure the Harcourt Street train station were also a failure. Captain McCormick had ordered Sergeant Frank Robbins and three men to barricade both ends of Hatch Street for a day and so cut off one means of access to the Green. To build the barricade, they commandeered a White Heather Laundry van and also raided a garage on Earlsfort Terrace for motor cars, despite the protests of the staff. At the station, the train to Wexford was delayed for four hours until Constance issued a permit for it to run. The rebels then moved back to the Green and ordered a man driving a dairy cart to back up against the gates facing Leeson Street. An attempt to take over a tram backfired when the driver went into reverse and escaped.

At the Green, many of the women initially assigned to first-aid stations and to the commissary were pressed into service. They patrolled the Green and found a few stragglers, including a clergyman and a young woman who became quite hysterical. Mary Hyland and Kathleen Cleary had taken over the summer house and had laid out sandwiches, ham, cheeses and cakes to feed the insurgents. To the casual onlooker, it was a bizarre sight – the men in uniform swinging their pickaxes and spades to make trenches and the women laying out food for a picnic. During the afternoon, members of the Volunteers arrived, looking to join the fight. Three Cumann na mBan women – Nora O'Daly, Bridget

Murtagh and May Moore – had arrived at the Green on their way to Jacob's factory. Not quite knowing what to do, they met Constance, who brought them to the summer house where Madeleine ffrench-Mullen was in charge of first aid. They decided to stay. Also arriving during the afternoon was Nellie Gifford and Liam Ó Briain, a 2nd Battalion man, who joined the St Stephen's Green force and spent the day digging a three-foot deep trench at the Leeson Street gate. It was soon pretty clear that taking the Green without securing at least one of the surrounding buildings had been a mistake.

Standing on the west side of St Stephen's Green was the Royal College of Surgeons in Ireland – a granite fortress of a building that was closed for the holiday weekend. A few hours after the Green was occupied, Mallin ordered Constance, Frank Robbins and ten others to search the college for rifles and ammunition belonging to the Officers' Training Corps. As Mallin unlocked a gate opposite the college, he noticed that the caretaker of the college was at the front door, attempting to get rid of Dr John Knott, an elderly fellow of the college who liked to spend his days in the library and, according to Robbins, 'was looking the worse for drink'. Mallin had told Constance and her group to veer left as if they were going to York Street so that the caretaker would not suspect their plan. As they passed it, Robbins sprinted for the main door, ordering the others to follow him. When Robbins reached the top step, a shot rang out, whizzing past his ear and hitting the top right-hand corner of the door, which the caretaker was attempting to slam shut. Robbins threw his full weight against the door and it gave a few inches. He jammed his foot in the gap and put the muzzle of a gun to the caretaker's throat.

When the caretaker professed no knowledge of the officers' corps or where they might find guns, Robbins was all for roughing him up until Constance took control. She ordered the caretaker, with wife and child, to be locked in their own bedroom. They protested mightily and banged on the door for some time, but finally went quiet. The rebels set about searching the building, with no success. When a supply of bombs arrived from Mallin, Constance and her group went to the roof of the building and awaited further orders. From the roof, they could see a woman on a bicycle waving to them. It was Margaret Skinnider, who brought them a tricolour that, despite a struggle with the rotting runners of the flagpole, was soon flying proudly over the college. On the street, the rebels were kept busy with a number of local women, mostly wives and relatives of Irishmen serving in the British army, who attacked them at every opportunity.

Constance found that she was too tired and excited to sleep that first night. She walked about looking for shelter and tried lying in one of the trenches. Because it was a cold, damp night, the ground was chilly, so she resumed walking until she noticed Dr Lynn's car, by then part of a barricade. She climbed in, found a rug and went to sleep in comparative comfort. Other members of the small force huddled under trees or stretched out on benches inside the Green, while the first aid and dispatch women slept on the floor of the summer house, a building that had no walls but did have a roof. When morning came, Constance could not forgive herself for having slept in comfort all night. She had intended to sleep only for an hour or so before giving up her place to someone else, but she woke only at 4am when a hail of machine-gun bullets hit the roof of the car.

On the second day, Hanna Sheehy Skeffington and members of the Irish Women's Franchise League arrived at the Royal College of Surgeons laden with food. Despite her husband's pacifism, Hanna was broadly supportive of the Rising. The couple had walked into Dublin's city centre where Hanna had stopped at the GPO to offer her assistance as a messenger. One of the first people she met was her priest uncle, Father Eugene Sheehy, an old-style Fenian and believer in physical force. After speaking to Connolly, Hanna was sent to St Stephen's Green. Constance remembered noticing some women approaching:

> Just then the leading figure approached and asked for Commandant Mallin. Some of us recognised the voice. It came from the lips of Hanna Sheehy Skeffington, who was struggling under the weight of a huge sack bulging out in queer shapes and completely concealing her. She was followed by more laden figures. They proved to be members of the IWFL ... and had collected a store of all manner of eatables from their friends ... to bring them to us though the bullet-swept streets. We had great fun unpacking the parcels and hearing who had contributed this ham or that tin of salmon or soup before we sat down and had a glorious meal.

Securing the overlooked spaces of St Stephen's Green was always going to be a problem. In all, there were 138 men and women in the Green, of whom about 103 men and fifteen women were members of the Irish Citizen Army. The remaining twenty or so were Volunteers. On Monday night, while the small rebel force huddled together to stay warm, British troops made their way up Kildare Street and into the Shelbourne Hotel by a side entrance, unheard and unobserved. Soon the front door to the hotel was barricaded with mattresses and soldiers were stationed at every window facing the Green, where the trees offered little in the way of protection.

At daybreak on Tuesday 25 April, it was not only Constance who was awoken by the sharp rattle of machine-gun fire from the roof of the hotel. Mallin and his troops, along with the women in the summer house, were forced to run for safety from the trench opposite the Shelbourne Hotel to the south-west corner of the Green, where the shrubs, trees and an embankment offered some protection. Mallin then sent Skinnider to the GPO with a dispatch; he realised at once that they would have to evacuate the Green. When Skinnider returned from the GPO, she was sent to bring in the sixteen men guarding the Leeson Street bridge before they were cut off, although the post could have proved its worth when British troops started marching into Dublin from the ferry in Kingstown. She cycled as fast as she could with bullets rattling the metal rim and the spokes of her wheels and puncturing a tyre.

All the rebels were, by then, retreating in twos and threes to the Royal College of Surgeons. In St Vincent's Hospital, Dr Louis A.D. Courtney later recalled hearing the faint sounds of 'A Soldier's Song' as it floated across the Green in the early morning. One young Citizen Army soldier was killed while retreating and, contrary to all humanitarian rules, the first aid women in their white frocks with big red crosses were fired on, with bullets tearing through one woman's skirt and knocking the heel off another's shoe. Five bodies were left in the Green, along with food, provisions and equipment. That more were not killed was a miracle. While Skinnider was reporting back to Mallin, a bullet whizzed through his hat: 'He took it off, looked at it without comment, and put it on again.' On the roof of the college, Michael Doherty lay slumped over the parapet, his blood staining the stonework. He was rescued by

Joseph Connolly, a brother of Seán Connolly. The two prisoners held in the Green were taken to the Royal College of Surgeons. One of them, W. Hopkins Ashmore, later reported that Constance was profuse in her apologies to the prisoners, explaining that their detention was for the cause of Ireland. She was not so calm when one officer they had released reported back to his superiors on everything he had seen, despite a promise that he would not do so.

By 7am, everyone was safely inside the Royal College of Surgeons. They rolled themselves up in rugs and slept. Later that day, with no police on the streets to stop anyone, looting broke out in the city, particularly in Sackville Street, where the Dublin poor climbed through the smashed windows of shops such as the branch of Noblett's confectionary shop, Saxone shoes and Lawrence's toy shop to scoop up armloads of sweets, toys and shoes. Excited children ran around playing 'rebels' and firing imaginary guns; an improvised game of golf took place in Sackville Street.

By now, 20,000 British soldiers had arrived in Dublin and martial law was proclaimed by Sir Matthew Nathan. Inside the college, the insurgents were well protected by the thick walls of the three-storey building. On the ground floor were lecture rooms and a museum; the classrooms and laboratories, as well as the library and boardroom were one storey up. On the third floor were the caretaker's quarters and a kitchen; Mallin and Constance used the caretaker's two rooms as offices. One end of a classroom on the second floor was curtained off and used as a first-aid room. Windows were barricaded with furniture and books. In all parts of the college, the smell of chemicals was all-pervasive and the presence of glass bottles containing unspecified parts of the human body were unnerving.

Nellie Gifford was put in charge of cooking, but could produce nothing in the way of hot food until she acquired a bag of oatmeal. Keeping the rebels fed was a problem at all the outposts, although those in Bolands had a plentiful supply of bread, flour and fruit cake and the Jacob's battalion gorged themselves on biscuits and cream crackers. At the GPO, bacon and eggs were available at the Pillar Café for anyone brave enough to make a break for it.

Constance was a whirlwind of activity, searching for anything that might be of use and offering advice and encouragement. She acted as a strict chaperone for the 150 men and twenty women who were living under the same roof, making regular inspections. There was intermittent firing on the college during the week and sniping from the rebels installed on the roof – except at midday, when a brief truce allowed the St Stephen's Green park keeper to feed the ducks.

On the north side of the Green, the United Services Club and other buildings were occupied by the British forces. Mallin organised groups to break through the walls from house to house on both the north and west sides of the Green. The original plan was to set fire to the buildings on the north side in an attempt to shift the British troops, but just before 10pm, when the fires were to be started, Constance crawled through the walls with an order from Mallin to stop.

Food was running out. Early in the week, Mary Hyland had left the park and, finding a milkman on his rounds, ordered him to hand over a can of milk. In similar fashion, Lily Kempson held up a bread cart with a revolver and Nellie Gifford acquired sacks of flour. When these provisions ran out, they began looting nearby houses and shops, finding bread, cheese and Oxo cubes. Mary McLoughlin made the hazardous journey to the GPO to explain to Connolly that the garrison was short of food and ammunition. He gave her £80 to bring to Michael Mallin, who refused it. They needed food and ammunition, not cash.

The garrison's only female casualty was Margaret Skinnider, who had spent Wednesday on the college roof. Seeing the damage at the Shelbourne Hotel that had been caused by the machine gun, she suggested cycling over to the hotel and lobbing a bomb attached to an eight-second fuse through one of its bow windows. The time lapse would allow her to escape before the bomb exploded; or so she argued. Mallin deflected her from this plan with an alternative job. On the roof of the University Church, on the Green's south side, was another machine-gun post and, to cut off the British soldiers in that post, Mallin wanted to burn out two buildings situated behind the Russell Hotel on the corner of Harcourt Street. He delegated Skinnider, William Partridge and three men to deal with one building. When they reached the building, Partridge smashed open its glass door with his rifle butt. The British opened fire, hitting Skinnider on her right side with three bullets. Partridge lifted her up and carried her to the street, where she saw Fred Ryan, aged only seventeen, lying in a pool of blood.

With help, she managed to walk to the corner and then Partridge and another man carried her back to the Royal College of Surgeons.

They laid her out on a large table, where she burst into tears not from the pain but because they had to cut away her fine uniform, supplied by Constance. When she refused to be evacuated to hospital, Madeleine ffrench-Mullen removed the bullets, with Constance standing by holding her hand. She was bandaged up and given a cot to sleep in. Later, Liam Ó Briain gave her a nightdress he had found in a nearby flat.

Soon after, Constance and William Partridge disappeared. When they returned, Constance quietly said: 'You are avenged my dear.' They had gone to where Fred Daly lay, and to attract the fire of the soldiers across the street, Partridge had stooped over the dead boy to lift him. There were only two soldiers and they both fired, giving Constance a chance to sight them. She fired twice and hit both. Or so she told Skinnider, who was soon in a delirious state, moaning and talking incoherently.

To keep fear at bay, many of the Catholic rebels turned to prayer. Constance was particularly impressed by the humility and gentle nature of William Partridge, who led the prayers of the rosary each night in the college. She asked to join in, and later dedicated her poem 'The Rosary College of Surgeons' to him.

That day, the gunboat *Helga* sailed up the Liffey and the boom of shelling was heard all over the city when it fired at Liberty Hall, which, unknown to the British, was by then empty except for the caretaker. Later, the sound of shelling became more frequent when heavy artillery was used against the GPO. At night, the sky glowed red with incendiary shells. From their post, members of the Royal College of Surgeons' garrison could hear the spatter of rifle fire at Mount Street Bridge, where a British contingent, marching into the city from Kingstown, came under fire from three outposts manned by Volunteers from Bolands Mills. After a day and night of fierce fighting, thirty British soldiers lay dead, with a further 157 wounded. Six Volunteers died.

On Thursday morning, to the rebels' delight, sixty-four rifles were found in the college. Word of other skirmishes came through. In north County Dublin, Volunteers made successful attacks on four Royal Irish Constabulary police barracks. In Ashbourne, County Meath, a bloody battle lasted for five hours. At the Magazine Fort in the Phoenix Park, a group of Fianna boys, pretending to play football, almost succeeded in blowing up the explosives held in the fort. When they failed to find the key to the high-explosives room, the disappointed boys set fire to the building. One soldier and a civilian died, with at least one Fianna boy wounded. Against all the odds, the Easter edition of *Workers' Republic* was published that day with a rousing poem called 'Our Faith' by Constance replacing the regular Irish Citizen Army column.

There was heavy fighting at the South Dublin Union, which, from its position off James' Street, controlled Kingsbridge Station, the terminus for trains from the Curragh military camp. From the Union, the rebels hoped to block southside approaches to the Four Courts. Cumann na mBan's Margaretta Keogh was shot dead when she rushed to help a wounded Volunteer – the only female rebel to die during Easter week. At Marrowbone Lane and at the Mendicity Institute on the south quays both sides suffered casualties. British fire was concentrated on the GPO, and Sackville Street, from the Liffey bridge to the GPO, was reduced to smoking rubble. At the Four Courts, Seán Heuston, one of Constance's Fianna boys, held out from Monday to Wednesday, with much of the fighting taking place in the maze of streets surrounding the building. Little fighting occurred outside the capital. MacNeill's summons on the Sunday to call off the Rising had made it impossible. While Galway and Wexford saw some action, most Volunteers stayed at home.

Inside the Royal College of Surgeons, messengers came and went, bringing food and news. By holding the building, they had already done more than Wolfe Tone, Constance told the garrison members. A rumour began that they were to flee the college and head for the Dublin and Wicklow mountains where they would continue the fight using guerilla tactics; this is what Mallin had expected would happen.

By Thursday, the British had thrown a cordon around the city isolating the main positions held by the insurgents. The GPO was surrounded and Connolly badly wounded. His wife, Lillie, staying at Constance's cottage, could see the smoke and fire enveloping the city below. She had found one of the few newspapers printed that week and read in it that her husband was dead; Nora arrived at the cottage and reassured her that Connolly, though badly wounded, was still alive.

On Saturday, the Royal College of Surgeons' garrison prepared for a possible charge by the British by attempting to demolish the staircase. The rebels celebrated the arrival of food, including a side of bacon, unaware of the official surrender that had been negotiated between Pearse and Brigadier-General Lowe earlier that day. On Sunday 30 April, Elizabeth Farrell, a Cumann na mBan member who had carried details of the GPO garrison's surrender a day earlier, was driven to Grafton Street by a British army officer. From there, she walked to the College of Surgeons carrying a white flag and a surrender order. Pale-faced and nervous, she went to the side door of the college at York Street and asked for Commandant Mallin. When she was told that he was sleeping and that the next in command was Markievicz, she gave the surrender order to Constance, who was indignant. 'Surrender? We'll never surrender!' she said, before waking Mallin with the news. A call went out for all the rebels in the Green area to report to the college immediately. Initially, there was a mixture of anger and excitement at the news. Constance argued that it would be better for them all to be killed at their posts. An exhausted Elizabeth Farrell became increasingly excited as the discussions continued, saying that the soldiers outside would blow her head off if she did not come out soon.

Once the rebels were all assembled, Mallin read the surrender order and he, Constance and Partridge each spoke of a job well done. An ambulance came to collect Skinnider and bring her to hospital. Her last words with Constance concerned a will, which Constance had slipped into the lining of Skinnider's coat with instructions to see that it got to her family. Mallin and Constance then led the group through the side door of the college, where they surrendered to Captain de Courcy Wheeler of the Kings' Royal Rifle Corps. After smartly saluting the captain, to whom she was related by marriage, Constance kissed her revolver before giving it up. 'I am ready' she said. Her flamboyant gesture may have been designed to distract attention from Mallin, a family man with four children and another on the way, who was well aware of his responsibilities as a provider, and had never planned on dying for Ireland. Constance refused de Courcy Wheeler's offer of transport to Dublin Castle and marched with Mallin and her comrades down Grafton Street and left into Dame Street.

Crowds lined the streets and one woman who waved encouragingly at Constance was arrested and spent over a week in jail. Constance's breeches came in for much comment. Most of the crowd waved hats and Union Jacks at the Staffordshire Regiment escorting the prisoners and yelled 'shoot the traitors' and 'mad dogs' at the rebels. Particularly virulent were the 'separation women'; because the GPO was destroyed, they would not get their allowance that month.

After a brief stop in the yard of Dublin Castle, the company set off for Richmond Barracks in Inchicore, where they were given tea and biscuits. Nora O'Daly carried the Red Cross flag throughout the march but, at the entrance to the Barracks, a soldier snatched it from her hands. Constance and Madeleine ffrench-Mullen were separated from the rest of the women. Once inside, Constance saw a number of women from the GPO and the Four Courts, among them Julia Grennan, who had spent Saturday night in a small park near the Rotunda. She ran over to shake hands and ask for news of others, but was bustled away.

Later in the evening, the company marched to nearby Kilmainham Gaol, a grim prison that had housed a long list of Irish rebels, among them Charles Stewart Parnell. With Constance was the medical student Brigid Lyons, who had been part of the Four Courts garrison. It was dark when they arrived, the gloom relieved only by the flickering candles carried by soldiers. Nora O'Daly saw Constance once again. She was on an upper landing smoking a cigarette when the other women were brought up. 'Put out that fag,' a guard shouted at her. When she refused, he knocked it out of her hand. She ignored him and smiled encouragingly at the other women before being put in a separate cell. O'Daly wondered at her self-control.

The rebellion was over. On the British side, including the military, the Royal Irish Constabulary and the Dublin Metropolitan Police, 120 were killed and 392 were wounded or missing. Of the rebels, an estimated 64 were killed, including nine at the GPO, six at St Stephen's Green and five at City Hall. A further 116 civilians died. The high casualty rate among civilians was blamed on their foolhardy curiosity.

Vindictiveness caused other fatalities, with fifteen civilians shot or bayonetted in their homes, allegedly by the British, during military operations in the North King Street area; some were killed even after the surrender of the GPO. The most shocking deaths occurred on

Wednesday 26 April, when Francis Sheehy Skeffington and two loyalist journalists were shot on the orders of Captain Bowen-Colthurst. Sheehy Skeffington was picked up on Tuesday evening when walking home after attempting to stop the looting in the city centre, while the two journalists were arrested when Bowen-Colthurst raided what he thought was a republican pub. The trio witnessed a rampage of violent behaviour from Bowen-Colthurst, including the shooting dead of an unarmed seventeen-year-old boy called J.J. Coade who was returning from church on the Rathmines road. On Wednesday morning, the captain suddenly ordered his men to execute the three men, possibly because of what they had witnessed.

Bowen-Colthurst's actions caused outrage, although army headquarters at Parkgate initially defended his behaviour. Thanks only to the determined actions of Dublin-born Major Francis Fletcher Vane, along with lobbying by Eva and Josslyn Gore-Both, Bowen-Colthurst was found guilty but insane by a military court on 16 May. Sheehy Skeffington, a pacifist, became the first martyr of the 1916 Rising.

CHAPTER TWELVE

Condemned to Live

Initially, the citizens of Dublin, far from sharing in the dreams and ideals of the rebels, turned against them for ruining their city and disrupting their lives. The trams had stopped running and, with both Bolands and Jacob's bakeries seized, bread was scarce. Shops were emptied of food and, for two days, no newspapers were published, making rumour the sole source of information. More crucially, the Irish, by and large, supported Britain in the world war then raging, with at least 150,000 signing up for the British army, as well as many more from the Irish community in Britain. Despite that, as the week wore on, the courage of the rebels and the fair-minded manner in which they treated civilians won them sympathy.

With a bitter and bloody war raging on the Continent, Army top brass were determined that the Irish rebels would pay for their cheek. When the chief secretary, Augustine Birrell, resigned in the immediate wake of the Rising, General Sir John Maxwell was sent to Ireland. Using the excuse of a possible connection with 'German intrigue and propaganda', Maxwell declared the Rebellion 'treason in time of war', punishable by death. As a military man, fresh from the failed invasion of Gallipoli, the political implications of his decision did not enter his head.

On 3 May, Patrick Pearse, Tom Clarke and Thomas MacDonagh were marched into a small courtyard at Kilmainham Gaol and shot by a firing squad. A day later, it was the turn of Edward Daly, Joseph Mary Plunkett, Michael O'Hanrahan and William Pearse, whose only crime was that he was the brother of Patrick. Because the male prisoners were held in the floor above the women, they could hear the priest when he came to the cells for a final call.

Alone in her damp Kilmainham cell, Constance lay awake, waiting for the morning when the door would clang open and she would be marched out to face the firing squad like her comrades. When a prison chaplain, certain that she would be shot, suggested that she wear a dress instead of her military uniform, Constance answered: 'I fought in these clothes and I'll die in them.'

In London, her sister Eva thought she was already dead; newspapers reported that her body had been found in St Stephen's Green. Her brother Josslyn noted in his diary for Sunday 30 April that the rebels had surrendered; a day later, he writes tersely 'No news'. On Tuesday, he drove to Annaghmore and asked the local MP, Charles O'Hara, to write to the Lord Lieutenant Lord Wimbourne on his sister's behalf.

On the morning of 4 May, Constance was taken from her cell and brought to a preliminary hearing presided over by Sir Alfred Bucknill, the deputy judge advocate-general – a 'fuzzy little officer with his teeth hanging out to dry'. Walter McKay, the seventeen-year-old page boy working at the University Club on St Stephen's Green, said that he had seen Constance drive up to the Green in a motor car, blowing her whistle and leaning out to give orders to a 'Sinn Féiner' after he had shut the gate of the Green.

> She then drove towards the Shelbourne Hotel – I saw her again about 1.15pm. She was then behind one of the monuments in the Green, she had a pistol in her hand which she pointed towards the club and fired. I ran upstairs and saw where the bullet struck. After firing she walked up towards the Shelbourne Hotel dressed in knickers and puttees.

The only other witness was Captain Henry de Courcy Wheeler who had accepted the surrender of the rebels at the Royal College of Surgeons. He described 'the accused' as armed with a pistol and ammunition in a Sam Browne belt. Bucknill later wrote that Constance broke down and cried. 'We dreamed of an Irish Republic and thought we had a fighting chance,' she had said. Her tears, Bucknill wrote, were 'a natural reaction to stress and disappointment'. It may be this hearing that William Wylie, the prosecutor for the trial, remembered when he described Constance as a broken woman pleading for her life who disgusted him. His account is at odds with all the available evidence.

A formal court martial was held later the same day, with more witnesses called. Although, like the other rebels, Constance had no legal representation, she was allowed to question witnesses. She made short work of the page boy, demonstrating that he could not have seen what he claimed from the University Club. When Constance asked him where he had been to school, and he revealed that he had been in an industrial school, he burst into tears when she then asked him if he had been sent there for thieving or some other crime.

Dr Charles de Burgh Daly, the man aimed at by Constance when he stood by the window of the University Club, told his story. He described her as wearing 'a man's uniform, green with a brown belt, and feathers in her hat'. At about one o'clock, she 'leaned up against the Eglington monument and took a deliberate pot shot at me in one of the open windows of the University Club. I was ... in uniform and the distance was about 50-60 yards. She could not tell that I was a doctor but, I suspect, considered I was a combative officer as I had ribbons on'.

Daly added that he had no knowledge of her killing anyone and added that she mixed up 'kindness and killing in accordance with her convictions'. He hoped that one day she might use her talents for the real benefit 'of our country'. Constance herself was to say that she saw Daly 'retire in time' and that the bullet hit the top of the window. According to the official report of her court martial, released only in 2002, Constance later said: 'I went out to fight for Ireland's freedom and it doesn't matter what happens to me. I did what I thought was right and I stand by it.'

The next morning she waited in her cell, listening for a third time to the crack of British rifles in the yard below. It was the turn of Major John MacBride, the estranged husband of Maud Gonne, to face the firing squad, although Constance did not know this. That night, an English soldier, on guard outside her cell, waited until all was quiet and then unlocked the door and offered her a cigarette. He sat down to smoke with her and told her that Pearse, Clarke and MacDonagh had been shot the first day, Daly, Plunkett, O'Hanrahan and Willie Pearse on the second and MacBride that morning. She was sure she would be next. Marie Perolz had asked Constance after her trial whether she had heard any news. 'I have been sentenced to death,' she said, although as yet she had heard nothing official.

On 6 May, she was standing looking out of the small window of her cell when a young officer entered. Obviously uncomfortable, he read her the results of the court martial. Like most of the rebels, she had been found guilty of taking part in an armed rebellion and of waging war against His Majesty the King and attempting to cause disaffection among the civilian population. The sentence was: 'Guilty. Death by being shot. The Court recommend mercy for the prisoner solely and only on account of her sex.' The sentence would be commuted to penal servitude for life. It was signed by General J.G. Maxwell, convening officer, and C.J. Blackader, Brigadier-General, president of the court.

The young officer had mumbled his way through the sentence. Constance asked him to read it again more clearly. When he finished, her response was simple: 'I wish you had the decency to shoot me.' She had been condemned to live; spared to contemplate the implications of the failed Rebellion without her comrades-in-arms. Constance was probably unaware that her commandant during the Rising, Michael Mallin, had made an extraordinary statement at his court martial, claiming that Constance had ordered him to take command of the men at St Stephen's Green. Many did think – including her old friend Lady Fingall – that Constance was in charge and Mallin probably believed that the British would never execute a woman. The pair may have concocted the scheme together; when Mallin's fifth child was born, she was named Mary Constance.

A frequent visitor to Kilmainham was the Capuchin friar, Father Albert Bibby, who smuggled out lines of poetry and other writings scribbled by Constance on scraps of brown paper. These he transcribed into a notebook before sending the originals to Eva in London. In a letter to Gertrude Bannister, a cousin of Casement's, Constance described lying awake at daybreak clinging to a crucifix given to her by Father Albert while 'the English murdered our leaders'.

Constance probably owed her life to Edith Cavell. A year earlier, the Germans had executed the British nurse, provoking outrage, and the British did not want to make the same mistake. Eva, anxiously waiting for news in London, was convinced that the personal intervention of the prime minister, Harold Asquith, saved Constance's life. After she was sentenced, Constance was moved to Mountjoy and, from her cell as Prisoner Number B374, she could hear the newsboys calling on the street outside. On 8 May, Mallin, Ceannt, Colbert and Heuston were executed; Colbert and Heuston were among the original Fianna boys from the first *sluagh* at Camden Street. That same day, Laurence Ginnell was forcibly ejected from the House of Commons after accusing Asquith of murder. John Dillon of the Irish Parliamentary Party made a powerful speech, appealing to the prime minister to stop the executions: 'it is not murderers who are being executed; it is insurgents who have fought a clean fight however misguided'.

A day later, Thomas Kent was executed in Cork and then came the news Constance had most dreaded: on 12 May, James Connolly and Seán Mac Diarmada were shot. Connolly, probably dying from gangrene in the leg that had been shattered during the fighting, was propped up in a kitchen chair when he faced the firing squad. Constance wrote a poem in honour of her great friend and pledged on his 'murdered body' that she would dedicate the rest of her life to the causes they had espoused.

> You died for your country and left me here
> To weep – No! My eyes are dry
> For the woman you found so sweet and dear
> Has a sterner destiny –
> She will fight as she fought when you were here
> For freedom I'll live and die.

The three-verse poem was given by Constance to a wardress as a souvenir before she was moved to an English prison.

With the executions, General Maxwell had seriously miscalculated, as George Bernard Shaw pointed out in a letter to the *Daily News* published on 10 May. The Irish rebel leaders were prisoners of war, entitled to mercy. 'It is absolutely impossible to slaughter a man in this position without making him a martyr and a hero. The shot Irishmen will now take their places beside Emmet and the Manchester Martyrs in Ireland and nothing in heaven or earth can prevent it.'

While the Rebellion had initially failed to ignite the patriotism of the Irish, the drip-feed of information about the executions changed that. The heartlessness of the executioners, often taking two volleys, and the callous treatment of James Connolly inspired appalled revulsion, not only in Ireland but across the United Kingdom. On the night after Pearse's trial, General Blackader, one of the three military judges presiding over the courts martial, dined with the Countess of Fingall. In her memoirs she reports the General saying of Patrick Pearse: 'I have had to condemn to death one of the finest characters I have ever come across. There must be something very wrong in the state of things that makes a man like that a rebel. I don't wonder that his pupils adored him.'

In the shop windows of Dublin, postcards of the executed rebels were displayed prominently. With nationalist organisations forced underground, religion provided a focus for discontent. The first manifestation of the deep public feeling came at the month's mind for the dead leaders – a mass celebrated a month after a death. The first of these, in Rathfarnham, remembered Patrick and Willie Pearse. Others followed at Merchant's Quay, John's Lane and elsewhere, with those attending flaunting their rebel badges. All Souls' Day on 1 November provided another opportunity for public commemoration.

Ignoring the rising political temperature, the British military continued to make wholesale arrests. A further 137 were sentenced to penal servitude and twenty-three to prison with hard labour. By 1 July 1916, 3,149 men and seventy-seven women had passed through Richmond Barracks, with 1,862 detained without trial. Prison would become a university for spreading the doctrines of nationalism. As well as the ill-treatment of the prisoners and the incompetence of officers, the insolence of the military in the streets, looting by soldiers and foul language used to women was causing increased anger among the public. Pearse had achieved his objective: whatever about the Rising itself, the extreme response of the British gave Sinn Féin and the nationalist movement the boost it needed.

At Mountjoy, Constance was allowed visitors, and her sister Eva and Esther Roper travelled from London, sailing into Kingstown on 12 May. On a glorious spring morning, the two women got an inkling of what was to come when they witnessed hundreds of khaki-clad soldiers crowding around the gangplank of their ship. She and Esther took a taxi through shattered streets with a 'muddled, desperate look' and, after a brief visit to Eva's cousin, the writer Susan Mitchell, who had obtained permission for the visit, they travelled on to Mountjoy. Only then did

Eva notice the newspaper placards with the headline 'Execution of James Connolly' written on them in large letters.

Inside the jail, Constance, calm and smiling, appeared behind 'a sort of a cage' set into the wall of a bleak whitewashed room. 'Nobody who has not gone through the ordinary prison visit can realise how unsatisfactory it is, nor what a strain it is, to fling one's conversation across a passage with a wardress in it, to a head appearing at a window opposite,' wrote Eva later. Her only thought was whether Constance had heard that Connolly '- and Seán Mac Diarmada – had been executed that very day. It proved an unnecessary anxiety: 'she knew everything'.

With little time available, Constance rapidly told her sister about the shock and grief of the surrender, as well as the details of her court martial. She was worried about Agnes Mallin, in hiding and penniless, and gave Eva directions so that she could find her. She expressed her bewilderment at the execution of Francis Sheehy Skeffington, who did not even believe in fighting. She had little to say about her own treatment. She was a 'convict' and a 'lifer' and that was that. It had been splendidly worthwhile – for one glorious week, Ireland had been free. After twenty minutes, the 'oddly becapped head disappeared from the window'. Eva would not see her sister for another four months.

At Kilmainham, when she was sure she would be executed, Constance asked Father Ryan to be with her at the end. After she was reprieved and transferred to Mountjoy, she registered as Catholic, though she was Church of Ireland by birth. On that final night in the college, Constance had knelt with the others in prayer. Suddenly she had 'a vision of the Unseen'. It brought her peace. In Mountjoy, Father McMahon, the Catholic chaplain, found her attitude to her new faith puzzling and he discussed it with Hanna Sheehy Skeffington:

> She wants to be received into the Church, but she won't attend to me when I try to explain transubstantiation and other doctrines. She just says, 'Please don't trouble to explain. I tell you I believe all the church teaches. Now, father, please tell me about the boys.'

Constance had shocked the good father by referring to Lucifer as 'a good rebel', but Sheehy Skeffington suspected that she was teasing; it was part 'of her habit of leg-pulling of authority'.

Sheehy Skeffington reflected that Constance belonged to the church of St Francis of Assisi rather than to that of St Paul. 'The ritual and the ceremonies, the music and the beauty of the Catholic Church, its art and cultural background attracted the mystic in her.' Over her bed was a picture of da Vinci's Christ.

Four days after her sister's visit, Constance wrote her first letter from prison. It was full of instructions. She missed her dog Poppet – who appeared to be with Lillie Connolly – and gave her sister explicit instructions for closing up Surrey House, mentioning mothballs and starch, a collection of wigs and how to get into a locked desk without a key. In there, Eva might find a bank book and papers for recovering income tax. She obviously hoped to use her things again: 'I don't want anything thrown away.' There were bills to be paid and St Mary's to be rented out. 'I think my name should be suppressed and it should be let in yours.' She had left a bag in Liberty Hall, where her bicycle was probably 'knocking round'.

She wanted her old housekeeper, Bessie Lynch, and servant, Bridie Goff, looked after and the rent paid on the 'little hall' in Camden Street. After Constance's sentence was commuted, her brother, Josslyn, was appointed administrator of her affairs, to her annoyance. Constance had wanted Eva to do the job, as was clear from this letter, and when Eva failed to tell Josslyn of their sister's instructions, relations became strained. Constance sent a rambling letter to her brother with wild suggestions about what he should do to raise money from her investments. She also wanted her false teeth returned.

In her letters to Eva, she was determined to keep cheerful. 'The life is colourless, beds are hard, food peculiar, but you might say that of many a free person's life ... So darling don't worry your sweet old head.' Mountjoy was heaven compared to her later experiences of prison life. She described it in a letter from England:

> There was so much life in Mountjoy. There were seagulls and pigeons – which I had quite tamed. There were 'Stop Press' cries, little boys splashing in the canal and singing Irish songs shrill and discordant, but with such vigour. There was a black spaniel too with long silky ears, and a most attractive convict baby with a squint – and soft Irish voices everywhere. There were the trains

'Broadstone and North Wall trams' and even an old melodion and a man trying to play an Irish tune on a bugle over the wall!

By the time Eva and her friends visited Surrey House, it had been thoroughly ransacked, first by the military authorities and then by looters in search of souvenirs. The furniture was smashed, and papers, ornaments, books and pictures were strewn about, many of them trampled and destroyed. A box of lantern slides had been overturned and every single slide had been crushed. A beautiful leather dressing case had been slashed by a bayonet. The garden had been dug up in search of arms. Among the items confiscated were the letters from Canon Hannay about the underwear Constance should wear in *Eleanor's Enterprise*. Margaret Skinnider claimed that the soldiers 'had the effrontery' to sell the books, fine furniture and paintings they had looted on the street nearby. Severals paintings, including Casimir's *Bread*, were left behind.

When Eva left the house, she was mistaken for Constance by bystanders, but although this made Dublin a dangerous place for her, she and Esther Roper trawled the shattered streets the next day in an attempt to find Agnes Mallin. In Inchicore they finally met Father Ryan, who knew the whereabouts of Mrs Mallin's family; they eventually found her and gave her some money.

Rumours had begun circulating that Constance had shot dead an unarmed policeman on the first day of the Rebellion. Neither Eva nor Josslyn knew whether this was true. Nor did they know what had happened at the court martial. Eva wrote to her brother: 'Can you find out exactly what happened at the court martial? I only heard half from Con and we ought to know this to contradict the vile stories some people are making.' Josslyn began an energetic campaign of writing letters, firstly to the British army in Ireland, then to the Chief Secretary and finally to the War Office. They replied telling him he could obtain a copy of the court martial if he made a formal application, providing Constance did not object.

There were two more letters to Eva from Mountjoy, one in tiny writing on toilet paper smuggled out by a sympathetic apprentice warder from Wexford. She told Eva that 'alas!' she was being exiled to Aylesbury. On 3 August, Roger Casement was hanged in Pentonville Prison, London, despite a vigorous campaign by supporters, among them Eva and Alice

Stopford Green, to have him released. Eva had attended his trial on at least one occasion and helped organise a petition for presentation to King George V at Buckingham Palace. It was to no avail.

Constance repeated that she did not mind being in jail and that her only desire was 'to be of some use to those outside in the long tedious struggle with England'. She explained that she was not going on hunger strike 'as I am advised by comrades not to do so'. She asked Eva to try and get news to Casimir, stating that 'It would have to be very diplomatically done to evade the censor'. The second letter was scribbled on the back of an envelope and mentions her daughter: 'I am glad that M was amused and not shocked!'

On 7 August, Constance arrived at Aylesbury, a forbidding Victorian prison in Buckinghamshire, first opened in 1847 as a county jail and converted to a women's prison in 1890. The entrance was through double doors; the first door was always banged shut and locked before the second was opened. Inside was a mixed bag of petty thieves, prostitutes, swindlers and murderers. Political prisoners were rare. She had enjoyed the ferry journey across the Irish Sea, with a 'sunny porthole and a fresh breeze', reporting that her escort had never been to sea before and suffered from seasickness. When they arrived, she saw a big airship like a Zeppelin: 'I long so to fly!'

Constance was put in solitary confinement and she quickly got used to the routine. The day began at 6.30am when prisoners washed and dressed and then ate a breakfast of six ounces of bread and one pint of tea, usually cold, in their cells. Work followed, hard or soft or none at all, depending on the sentence. In Constance's case, it was hard labour and she got two ounces of cheese and a small piece of bread at ten o'clock to keep her going. Lunch at noon consisted of two ounces of meat, two ounces of cabbage, one potato, thick flour gravy and six ounces of bread. On Thursday this was changed to suet pudding with black treacle. On Fridays there was fish instead of meat. Supper at 4.40pm was a pint of cocoa or tea and six ounces of bread. At 5.30pm, the prisoners were locked up for the night. During her sentence, Constance's weight dropped from a healthy eleven stone to a gaunt seven and a half stone.

Although her fellow prisoners were 'the gutter rats of England', Constance described 'a certain community of hatred that gave one mutual interests and the mutual sport of combining to pinch onions, dripping or rags!' The prisoners were perpetually hungry and always on the look-out for an extra turnip or onion. It kept them going, she said. She also commented: 'All prison does for people is to teach them to use bad language and to steal.'

Despite the cheerful tone she maintained in her letters to Eva, Constance hated being constantly observed though a painted 'eye' in the door of her cell and, in her first week at Aylesbury, she spent her nights awake and pacing. After some time, she was sent to the sewing room – the warmest room in the prison – where she made prisoners' nightgowns and articles of underwear from coarse unbleached calico. Because Constance had been entered in the record as Catholic, she was allowed to arrange the flowers for the chapel. The chaplain, Father Scott, won her affection for his goodness to even the most hopeless of prisoners. Prisoners were allowed one book a week and, after a few weeks, they were permitted to write one letter a month.

Staskou wrote to Josslyn in August. Like most of the family, he regarded the Easter Rising as a 'sad stupid business' and added that it was a blessing that his stepmother 'cannot get into more trouble'. Since the censors prevented Constance and Casimir from writing directly to each other, Casimir wrote to Josslyn in September from Kiev, treading very carefully around the subject of his wife and asking for news of the entire family. Constance was concerned about Casimir and Staskou, believing that very few of her letters to them ever got through and exasperated at having to deal with her husband's many creditors. She suggested to Josslyn that now he had found an address for Casimir, he should send all his bills on to him; Josslyn had been covering his brother-in-law's debts. In another letter, she asked Josslyn to send on a photograph of her daughter Maeve, whom she thought was too young to visit her mother in jail.

Constance started sewing, stealing a needle from the workshop and pulling coloured threads from rags for use as embroidery cotton. From these meagre offerings, she fashioned things of beauty, rising early to sew and then hiding away her precious pieces of cotton. Among the small items she made was a pincushion embroidered with the words 'Easter Week 1916' along with her initials worked with her own hair. It became the prized possession of a prison nurse originally from Galway. After an embroidered picture of the Madonna and child was found in her library book, her cell was searched and the needle and rags were confiscated.

Whatever about sewing for herself, sitting still for hours in the sewing room did not suit Constance's restless spirit and she asked to be moved. Her next job was cleaning the prison kitchen, where she became an expert at scrubbing floors – an art she would later demonstrate to Kathleen Clarke, though initially she proved so bad at this routine task that she was ordered to start again. This she did without grumbling; prisoners who complained risked being certified as insane and sent to Broadmoor Criminal Lunatic Asylum. She was determined to be a model prisoner and, apart from her undercover sewing, on only one other occasion did she rebel. When the Germans were making a successful push, the prisoners were ordered to go to the chapel and pray for the success of the British troops. Constance, along with a German spy and an Irish-born swindler called Mary Sharpe, refused to do so. Sharpe, originally from County Longford, and better known as the notorious 'Chicago May', would later write her memoirs. She remembered Constance as the 'grandest' woman she had ever met and admired her for her courage. 'No kind of hardship ever fazed her,' she said.

When the women refused to pray, they were punished, wrote Sharpe:

> For spite, they made the three of us women carry enough gruel around the prison to feed the entire 200 convicts. We had to carry immense, heavy cans up winding stairs. While we were doing this, the Countess recited long passages in Italian from Dante's *Inferno*. The place looked like Hell, all right, with the lights dimmed and musty-smelling bags tacked across the windows, as a precaution against bombing.

Constance was to criticise the prison service strenuously, arguing that it only bred criminals and should be abolished. She painted a graphic picture of the dirt and filth endured by all prisoners. Dinner was served in rusty old cans, with no facility for washing them. Along with another convict, she did her best by using a bowl on a kitchen table and towels. Often the water was cold and there was no washing powder or soda.

I could give you endless examples of English cleanliness. It may be summed up as follows: Brasses, floors, doorknobs, all that jumps to the eye immaculate, but dirt and carelessness behind the scenes. I have seen vermin found in the baths.

Because she was a 'Star Class' prisoner, she could associate only with others in this class. Of the twenty-six women in Aylesbury at the time, twelve were serving sentences for wilful murder, three for manslaughter and one for woundings. All worked in the kitchen. In an article about her time at Aylesbury, which was published later, Constance criticised the then governess – Dr S.F. Fox – as possessing neither heart nor imagination. She described the filth of the conditions, the constant fear of picking up 'loathsome diseases' and the disturbed mental state of many prisoners. One section of the prison contained 150 prisoners, and their food tins were often returned to the kitchen in a state too disgusting to describe. One of the 'girls' in the 'Borstal section' tried killing herself by cutting her throat while another set fire to her cell and nearly died of the burns. Several tried to hang themselves with the rope used for making mailbags; others swallowed buttons and huge needles. 'Poor girls! It seemed so wicked and futile to drive them to this.'

While Constance kept herself scrupulously clean, she was not particularly tidy. Because she had lost so much weight, her skirt had to be hitched up, with the two sides rarely even. Her blouse hung out and there were glimpses of a grey petticoat. Prison cells did not contain a mirror. Talk was forbidden and the lack of companionship proved the greatest of hardships for Constance. 'Even the miserable little grain of comfort you can get from a few minutes' talk with another prisoner can only be procured by endless trickery and deceit.'

The Irish male prisoners of the Rebellion had won the right to associate with other prisoners for an hour each day, but this privilege was not extended to Constance and the five other Irish women deported to England. Marie Perolz and Brigid Foley spent time in Aylesbury but had left before Nell Ryan, Winifred Carney and Helena Molony arrived. As internees, they were held in a different wing of the prison to Constance. Twice a day they would stand on a high step and wave across a wall as she passed on the way to the small wash-house. They also saw her in church on Sundays and occasionally smuggled her a note of greeting.

In August 1916, the committee and members of Cumann na mBan elected Constance president at their annual convention. This was more than a gesture; with so many men in jail, it was left to women to argue the case for Ireland and its prisoners internationally. A number of women travelled to the USA, among them Min Ryan, Nellie Gifford, Nora Connolly and Hanna Sheehy Skeffington, who brought with her a letter for President Woodrow Wilson. This was signed by, among others, Margaret Pearse, Jennie Wyse Power, Louise Gavan Duffy and Mary Colum, as well as Constance in her capacity as president of Cumann na mBan. It put forward Ireland's claim for self-determination and appealed to Wilson to include Ireland among the small nations for which the United States was fighting.

During the autumn of 1916, the other Irish women at Aylesbury asked for a move to the same wing as Constance. They were prepared to give up all their privileges, including visits, food and letters, to do so and undertook not to communicate further with the outside world. Their request was 'disallowed'.

Constance remained resilient; she was determined not to let prison break her and she kept her letters to Eva upbeat. Her first letter from Aylesbury, dated 8 August 1916, was closely written on two sheets of an official form. There were strict rules when it came to correspondence. Prisoners could write only to a 'respectable friend', watching their language and sticking to personal matters, with no mention of politics and no complaints allowed. The letters were censored.

She wrote that she had recently seen herself in a mirror – thin and sunburned with her teeth turned black. Compared to Mountjoy, Aylesbury was 'queer and lonely'. She found it difficult to understand what anyone said to her. She was impressed by the garden, with its hollyhocks and a 'great crop of carrots'. This she passed every day when they exercised going 'round and round in a ring – like so many old hunters in the summer'.

She had dreamt of her sister a few nights before and remarked that she dreamed a great deal in prison. She asked Eva when her next book was coming out, 'the one with some of my pictures'. She regretted that they 'were very bad' and that she could do much better now. 'I was just getting some feeling into my black and white when I left Ireland. I made quills out of rooks' tail feathers that I found in the garden, they are much nicer than most pens – you can get such a nice soft line.' She tells Eva not to worry about her. 'I am quite patient and believe that everything will happen for the best.' The letter was signed 'Yrs Con- (vict G12)'.

The book she referred to arrived a few weeks later. It was *The Death of Fionavar*, a verse play describing the 'world-old struggle in the human mind between the forces of dominance and pity, of peace and war'. Over the winter of 1915–16, Constance had decorated it with borders of primroses, birds, lilies, butterflies, cocoons and winged horses – a favourite symbol for both sisters. The book was dedicated 'To the Memory of the Dead. The Many who died for Freedom and the One who died for Peace'.

In Eva's poem in honour of the rebels, she writes:

> Poets, utopians, bravest of the brave,
> Pearse and MacDonagh, Plunkett, Connolly,
> Dreamers turned fighters but to find a grave,
> Glad for the dream's austerity to die.
>
> And my own sister, through wild hours of pain,
> Whilst murderous bombs were blotting out the stars,
> Little I thought to see you smile again
> As I did yesterday, through prison bars.

Shortly after, Eva received a few unauthorised letters, undated and unsigned, written on toilet paper. Constance had found 'a real friend' who was taking 'awful risks' for her, bringing titbits of news and 'tuck'. She asked Eva to meet her and to find someone with 'not too grand an address' who could act as an intermediary. She had learned the art of discretion. 'You had probably better not try and see her again, as most likely you are both under watchful and protective eyes.'

In a second illicit letter, Constance tells Eva that she had been moved back to the workroom and given sewing to do. She comments, 'Don't count on me getting out for ever so long. Unless a real fuss is made (home and America).' She thought that the trade unions should have an inspector or visitor in the jails. She loved the book with its dedication: 'I love being in poetry and feel so important!'

A third note was little more than a list of questions relating to conditions within the prison:

> These questions should be asked me and all political prisoners at a visit: What do you weigh? What was your normal weight? What do you get to eat? Can you eat it? How much exercise do you get per day? How often do you get clean under-clothes? Are you constipated? Can you get medicine? What temperature is the room you work in? What is your task, i.e. how much must you do in a week?

In September, Constance had her first visit from Eva and Esther Roper. 'You don't know what a picture the two of you made, all nice soft dreamy colours. (Moral! Always visit criminals in your best clothes.)' The prison matron, E.W. Sharp, sat in on this visit and, in her report, she relayed a story that Constance told Eva of throwing a glove with a message inside it to friends when she was taken away from Mountjoy by taxi cab. Constance asked Eva to give Marie Perolz a certain dress that she was to wear like 'Elijah's Mantle'; an elliptical way of telling Perolz that she was to carry on her work. She asked Eva to find nineteen-year-old Lily Kempson, who had fought with her during the Rising and delivered messages to and from the GPO, describing her as her 'right hand' and one of her 'chief messengers'. She begged her to see her daughter Maeve and also asked Eva to contact the veteran Clan na Gael man John Devoy in the USA if help was needed.

A police report commenting on the matron's report confirmed that Constance had thrown her glove to three women standing on the corner of Berkeley Road immediately after she left Mountjoy in a taxi cab, but they had felt the gesture was merely 'bravado'. Lily Kempson (or Lizzie Anne Kempston as she was called in the report) had sailed for New York from Liverpool on 1 July en route to San Francisco. She would marry there and, when she died in 1996 at the age of ninety-nine, was the last remaining survivor of 1916.

Since there was so little news to report in her letters, Constance remembered old friends and family, wrote down pieces of verse and told of her dreams and anything beautiful she had noticed. Very little outside news filtered through to the prisoners, restricted as they were to occasional 45-minute visits. However, news of Constance and the other prisoners was trickling out. They may have been behind bars but their influence was spreading and the British authorities were well aware of this. It was one of the reasons they were not kept in London prisons, where their supporters could have gathered.

Although Asquith had been replaced by David Lloyd George as head of a coalition government in December 1916, Sir Edward Carson remained in the cabinet as First Lord of the Admiralty and wielded considerable influence. In the House of Commons, John Dillon had brought up the question of the Irish prisoners several times and, by 21 December, Henry Duke, the chief secretary for Ireland, had decided it was time to free them. The following day, 600 untried prisoners were released from the Frongoch camp in Wales; among them was a young Michael Collins. More were released from Reading on 23 December and Winifred Carney and Helena Molony, the two untried women still in Aylesbury, were sent home on Christmas Eve. Despite efforts by the British authorities to keep the homecomings low key, the released prisoners returned home to bonfires and celebrations.

Constance was not released, despite a letter of entreaty to the Home Secretary written by Eva after her sister had served six months in prison: 'The fact of there being no legal limit to the terms of her imprisonment owing to the absence of any form of trial is a cause of great anxiety to her relatives and friends'. Captain Jack White wrote to Henry Duke on Constance's behalf: 'Constance Markievicz is one of my greatest friends and in many ways one of the finest women that ever breathed'. He argued that she should be removed to Lewes prison where she could associate with the other Irish prisoners: 'it's horrible to think of her in the surroundings she now is'.

In a letter she wrote at Christmas, Constance mentions her sorrow at the death of an old friend, Ernest Kavanagh, a caricaturist whose drawings had appeared regularly in the nationalist press. He had been killed by British fire while working in his office at the front of Liberty Hall on the Tuesday of Easter week. Constance had only just heard of his death.

She was thrilled with the forty-six Christmas cards she had received and, by way of a return Christmas greeting, she drew a picture of a woman behind bars, looking outwards. There were birds on the window ledge and in the air and a verse on either side of the picture.

On one side:

> The wandering winds at Xmas time
> The twinkling of the stars
> Are messengers of hope and love
> Defying prison bars.

On the other:

> The birds that fly about my cage
> Are vagrant thoughts that fly,
> To greet you all at Xmas time –
> They wing the wintry sky.

Her sister's card to her did not arrive until a week after Christmas, having caused some alarm at the Home Office. Eva had drawn a similar card, which Constance thought better than her own. She pictured a woman looking through a barred window at an angelic figure with a harp. Four children surrounded the singer, while on the border women sat, kneeled or stood.

The verse read:

> Do not be lonely, dear, nor grieve,
> This Christmas Eve
> Is it so vain a thing
> That your heart's harper, Dark Roseen,
> Crowned with all her sixteen stars,
> A wandering singer, yet a queen,
> Crowned with all her seventeen stars,
> Outside your prison bars
> Stands carolling?

The authorities thought the verse was code for a prison escape, although no such plan was ever concocted. Constance's letter of 29 December 1916 shows her extraordinary acceptance of her fate:

All my life in a funny sort of way seems to have led up to the last year, and it's all been such a hurry-scurry of a life. The great wave has crashed up against the rock and now all the bubbles and ripples and little me slip back into a quiet pool of the seas.

Constance was always delighted to see her sister, who usually brought Esther Roper with her. Roper marvelled at Constance's courage. She had even won over some of the prison staff. 'No prisoner was allowed to talk in the passages, but the first sound we heard while we waited was always her gay ringing laugh as she came along the corridor from the cells, talking to the wardress in charge of her.'

After a few weeks, Constance had been given a large notebook of cheap lined paper for sketching and jotting down verses. Each page was numbered so none could be torn out, and it was regularly censored. After a time, she got a second notebook of better-quality paper, which was unlined. On the first page of the original book was a sketch of a bookplate for her sister. That was followed by sixty pages of verse and many drawings, mainly images of Irish heroes or horses; she was good at horses. The second notebook contained mostly finished examples of the drawings from the first and illustrated poetry – her own, and her sister's. Two pictures show Joan of Arc kneeling with a sword in her left hand, rosary beads in her right and angels hovering.

Like Josslyn, Constance was a keen gardener and, even on her busiest days in Dublin, she had usually found time to tend to her garden. An attempt to grow a rose in her prison cell failed and when she told her sister, Eva wrote a verse:

There is nothing good, there is nothing fair
Grows in the darkness thick and blind
Pull down your high walls everywhere
Let in the sun, let in the wind.

On one of the last pages of the second book was another poem by Eva called 'To C.A.', which refers to St Francis. This Constance had illustrated with a striking picture of St Francis surrounded by birds and animals.

In Ireland, the provincial press, indifferent to the Rising when it happened, was now supportive. The *Sligo Champion*, which had pointedly ignored Constance's activities since 1911, commented sympathetically on her plight, and Sligo was one of many towns appealing for rebel prisoners to be better treated. At the behest of her family, the barrister J.F. Cunningham wrote a number of letters to Henry Duke asking for her release on health grounds. Since all 'the nationalists' had been released, he was 'begging this concession' on behalf of a family of unionists. He argued that, by holding the Irish internees, the British government was giving the Kaiser 'a trump card'. England was being 'placarded before Europe as inflicting a miserable fate on the people of Ireland'. When a peace conference assembled, the case of Ireland – a country England 'had no real quarrel with' – was sure to come up. In a later letter dated 26 January, he said, 'The Gore-Booths are no more rebels than I am, or than you are, or than Mrs Pankhurst, or Annie Kearney'. Cunningham was prepared to offer all his wealth 'and his head to boot' to guarantee her future good behaviour. Constance would have been horrified at the tone of his letters.

In January, Ernley Blackwell, the Undersecretary of State at the Home Office, writing from the Home Office in Whitehall, argued that it was impossible to organise a 'woman's side' at Lewes prison, since she would be the sole woman so accommodated. 'She has all the other privileges of the male prisoners and the length of her visits has been extended to three quarters of an hour'. He denied that she was living in the 'atmosphere and conversation of a brothel', as Eva had argued.

On 26 January 1917, Constance was visited by Esther Roper and Lady Clare Annesley, a feminist and pacifist from Castlewellan in County Down. She was now allowed daily visits. According to the principal matron's report, she told them that she had been accused of being in command of the army that attacked Dublin Castle, which was totally untrue. An unexpected visitor was Sir John Leslie, an admirer from years earlier, who brought her drawing materials. Other visitors included Alfie Byrne, later the Lord Mayor of Dublin, who interrupted her while scrubbing in the kitchen, and the Dowager Duchess of St Albans, who worried that she was not saying her prayers.

Alfie Byrne and Captain White, along with Eva and Esther Roper, continued to hound the authorities with petitions and questions in parliament about her status. Constance, because she was jailed at Aylesbury, was the only political prisoner in a British jail not allowed the privilege of association with comrades. With her health suffering, Eva finally gained for her the concession of a glass of milk a day. She was always hungry.

On 17 February 1917, Louie Bennett, on behalf of the Irishwomen's International League, sent a petition to the Home Secretary asking him to grant Constance the ordinary privileges of a political prisoner. On 25 February 1917, C.P. Scott of the *Manchester Guardian* raised Constance's case with David Lloyd George. He was unimpressed: 'a little solitary confinement will do her no harm'.

In a by-election held in Ireland that month, Count Plunkett, father of executed rebel Joseph, who was strongly supported by Sinn Féin and the Irish Volunteers, was elected MP for Roscommon. It was a first defeat for the Irish Parliamentary Party in the area for forty years and a bitter blow for John Redmond. In March, Eva received a letter from Father Albert Bibby of the Capuchin order who, as chaplain to the IRB Supreme Council, had ministered to the 1916 leaders before their executions at Kilmainham. He told Eva of a meeting called by Dublin's lord mayor to discuss the release of 'all our dear friends'. In April, the direction of the world war changed when the USA came in. The British were well aware of the anti-English beliefs of some twenty million Irish-Americans, many of them families starved out of their country during the Famine. Rumours that Markievicz was being ill-treated in prison were spreading in Irish-American circles.

A few weeks after the Americans entered the war, Count Plunkett called a convention in Dublin to formulate a programme for Irish independence. Among those on the organising committee were Arthur Griffith and Helena Molony. Delegates from seventy groups agreed to form a National Council to put forward Ireland's position at the peace conference they hoped would take place soon.

Eva continued her campaign to have her sister's prison sentence reduced, enlisting the help of friends, organisations and the press in both Ireland and England. They sent letters to town councils begging for support and suggested forwarding resolutions to the Home Office.

Questions were asked in the House of Commons and, in May, Cumann na mBan sent a series of letters to countries drawing attention to the treatment of the 122 Irish prisoners of war still jailed in English convict prisons. Constance's friend Æ wrote a tribute to the rebels, which he circulated privately:

> You, brave on such a hope forlorn,
> Who smiled through crack of shot and shell,
> Though the world cry on you with scorn,
> Here's to you, Constance, in your cell.

On 9 May, the Irish Parliamentary Party suffered another blow when Joseph McGuinness, then a prisoner in Lewes, won the South Longford by-election, beating the IPP candidate by thirty-seven votes. A month later, on 10 June, a large protest meeting on behalf of Irish political prisoners was held at Beresford Place and was addressed by Count Plunkett and Cathal Brugha. Lloyd George, anxious to reassure his new American allies that the British were attempting to solve the 'Irish problem', called for a convention in July to discuss Home Rule. Although Sinn Féin, supported by labour organisations, decided to ignore the convention, it did have one positive side effect. In order to promote an atmosphere of conciliation, Andrew Bonar Law, the leader of the House of Commons, announced on 15 June that all rebels held since the 1916 Easter Rising would be released.

A day later, the men were freed. At the gate of Pentonville, Éamon de Valera was handed a telegram telling him that he would be the Sinn Féin candidate for the West Clare by-election caused by the death of John Redmond's brother, Willie, in the war.

Constance's last letter from Aylesbury was dated 6 June. She wrote about a book on St Francis sent to her by Father Albert, of the decoration for a poem by Eva, about horoscopes and about spiritual communication with her sister at a certain time each day. She remembered how she had conducted meetings with 'the fun of bursting thro' all the red tape' and confessed that she was beginning to believe in anarchy.

On Sunday 17 June, Eva got a message from the Home Office; she could go to Aylesbury the next day and collect her sister. In a drawing expressing her joy, Constance showed an open cage, with the bird ready to fly with wings outstretched. The next morning, Eva and Esther Roper went to the prison, 'armed with all the gay clothes we could beg or borrow'. Soon Constance had cast off her prison clothing and, resplendent in a blue dress, she left Aylesbury prison for ever.

By the time the little group reached Eva and Esther's flat at 33 Fitzroy Square, crowds of journalists and well-wishers were waiting. Among them were Marie Perolz, Kathleen Lynn and Helena Molony who had taken the ferry to England as soon as they heard of Constance's pending release. In London, Constance enjoyed tea and strawberries on the terrace of the House of Commons with Eva, Esther, Alfie Byrne and Captain Jack White 'resplendent in top-hat and spats'. She graciously acknowledged the bows of her political enemies.

After three days of celebration and catching up, Constance was seen off at Euston Station by exultant supporters singing 'The Soldiers' Song' while she stood to attention. When the call came for three cheers, Constance kissed the bunch of roses she held in her arms and flung it into the crowd. At Holyhead, flag-waving supporters sang and cheered as she boarded the *MV Leinster*.

With Eva by her side, she arrived at Carlisle Pier in Kingstown late on the afternoon of 21 June. So many supporters were waiting that she struggled to get on the Dublin train. All along the ten-mile route, supporters lined the railway track. At Westland Row train station, her followers jostled one another to get a better view of their heroine, who was dressed in an old cardigan suit, topped by a magnificent new hat. Small boys climbed lamp posts. A great cheer and a display of republican flags greeted her when she took her place with Eva in Kathleen Lynn's car, driven by a uniformed Volunteer. She passed through the crowds, standing in the car, holding a large bouquet of flowers. A pipe band headed the procession, followed by representatives of all the organisations to which she had contributed.

From the station, the cavalcade moved along Great Brunswick Street and Tara Street before crossing Butt Bridge to Liberty Hall. The cheers continued when she walked up the steps and into the building. When she appeared at one of the windows, she had but a few words to say. 'I thank you more than I can say for the welcome back to Dublin that you have given me – I find Ireland rebel at last. We shall go on working until Ireland is free once again. I am going home now to rest in order that I may start work at once.' On her way to Dr Lynn's house in Rathmines, the car passed the GPO, the Royal College of Surgeons and Jacob's, all bearing the scars of the 1916 Rising. Outside Dr Lynn's house she spoke briefly, with a police observer carefully noting every word. 'I will now only say goodnight to you but we will meet again tomorrow or the next day and every day and we will all go on working until we die and until Ireland is a republic.'

When released, Constance had no home and no money. Ensuring that she had enough to live on was the union that she had so staunchly supported; she also received a generous £500 from the Irish National Aid Association and Volunteer Dependants' Association as well as money from Josslyn. Her daughter Maeve, now aged sixteen, was refusing to hear anything of her notorious mother. When sent to a small private school in New Milton, Hampshire, she was teased about her background.

There was only one thing left for Constance to do. On 24 June, she was formally received into the Catholic Church at Clonliffe College, taking the baptismal name of Anastasia. Among those present was Agnes Mallin. Joining the Catholic Church was Constance's way of identifying completely with the cause of Ireland. Casement was a convert to Catholicism for much the same reasons, as was Maud Gonne MacBride. Others thought differently: Dr Kathleen Lynn remained staunchly Church of Ireland all her life, while Rosamund Jacob, a Quaker, believed that the Catholic Church was one of the greatest influences for evil in the world.

Constance soon resumed her work with the labour movement. She was on the Irish Citizen Army executive and she raised money for the James Connolly Labour College. In 1917, with Helena Molony, Kathleen Lynn, Louie Bennett and Helen Chevenix, she was working to promote the rights of Irish women workers and was elected president of the Irish Women's Workers Union. Two strikes were settled by the union, although Constance was not involved. The nationalist cause remained her top priority.

CHAPTER THIRTEEN

Sinn Féin – We Ourselves

In the months following the Easter Rising, Irish nationalists grieved for their lost leaders. Replacing them would not be easy.

Friction between the various political groups opposing British rule was never far below the surface, with Arthur Griffith and Count Plunkett holding very different views. In early June 1917, a meeting was called to draw up a new unified republican policy. As well as Sinn Féin and the Irish Republican Brotherhood, the Liberty Clubs, the Irish Nation League, Plunkett's Mansion House Committee and the Released Prisoners' Organisation were represented. A leader emerged in the form of the American-born Éamon de Valera, the only commandant from the Easter Rising to have avoided the firing squad.

De Valera, tall and austere, was implacably republican and socially conservative. Born in the United States and brought up by his grandparents in Bruree, County Limerick, he took the Sinn Féin view that an independent Ireland must be protected from the corrupting influences of the British system and global industrialisation. The Roman Catholic faith of the Irish, he believed, not only distanced them from Britain but – as its name implied – formed a link between Ireland and a wider European community. While he respected the role of women in the political sphere, he believed that their roles as wives and mothers were paramount. During the Rising, when he commanded the brigade at Bolands Mills, he resolutely refused to have any women under his command.

De Valera made a dramatic start to his by-election campaign in County Clare by quoting the Easter Week Proclamation. A vote for de Valera, his election posters proclaimed, was 'a vote for Ireland a nation, a vote against conscription, a vote against partition, a vote for Ireland's language, and for Ireland's ideals and civilisation'. Against him, the Redmondites opted for Patrick Lynch, who was a crown prosecutor.

Constance, a big draw since her release from prison, was in Ennis on 7 July to support de Valera and address several meetings. There was no further need to call for a rebellion, she proclaimed, because Sinn Féin's policy was focused on gaining and using political power, backed by a strong Volunteer force, whose immediate duty was to keep order. At one meeting, with a number of soldiers' relatives in the audience, her rousing republicanism so provoked them that the leaders of the Labour League of Ennis were forced to rescue her. Although her clothes were torn and her hat bent, her spirits remained high.

De Valera won the seat for Sinn Féin, receiving 5,010 votes, compared to the 2,035 won by Lynch. After his victory, de Valera appeared on the steps of the courthouse in Ennis wearing his Volunteer uniform. Beside him were Constance, Count Plunkett and Arthur Griffith.

In the month following Constance's release from prison, the city of Kilkenny and her native Sligo both made her an honorary citizen. She was one of the few women ever so honoured and the occasions were a convenient excuse for Sinn Féin rallies. For the ceremony in Kilkenny on 19 July, Constance travelled by train with de Valera, Laurence Ginnell and William T. Cosgrave, the Sinn Féin candidate for the forthcoming by-election in the city.

The following week, Constance returned home to Sligo. When she wrote to fix a date, she acknowledged that she was overwhelmed by the honour. 'I long to see Sligo again. I used to think and dream of our hills and rivers and of the sun setting out over the sea and of all the people at home. My thoughts were often with you all this weary year I spent in an English jail.' She signed her name, followed by ICA (Irish Citizen Army) and q12, her Aylesbury convict number.

On the evening of Saturday 21 July, foghorns and cheers greeted the arrival of her train. A brass band played nationalist tunes, including 'Easter Week' and 'A Soldier's Song', and a torchlight procession brought her to the Sinn Féin hall on Teeling Street for a speech of welcome from the Mayor Councillor Dudley M. Hanley. Not everyone was pleased to see her; Sligo had its share of British sympathisers and anti-nationalists. A 'separation woman' charged at the group that was carrying the large Sinn Féin banner at the front of the procession and was hustled away. At Old Market Street, a group of women waved Union Jacks and indulged in 'very objectionable expressions'. One woman got a punch in the face when she tried to snatch the Sinn Féin banner. During the speeches, these women remained on the fringes of the group, booing and singing. A group of young men squared up to them, while the speakers on the platform appealed for calm. Sinn Féiners, for their part, felt 'insulted' by the large Union Jack fluttering over the Constitutional Club, the meeting place of the local Orange Order. Members of the Gore-Booth family kept their distance and the church at Drumcliff was the closest she got to Lissadell that weekend; she stayed in a local hotel.

In her speech of thanks, Constance told the crowd that they should not vote to send any man to Westminster 'to help England govern Ireland'. 'I cannot say many more words, as you will notice I am hoarse. That is what happens when you are kept in jail for a year and when you are allowed to speak only in a whisper.' Darrell Figgis, who had escorted her to Sligo, ended his speech by appealing to the crowd to disperse quietly.

After mass on Sunday morning, Constance spent the day addressing meetings in Drumcliff, Maugherow and Grange. The group had split up in order to attend as many meetings as possible in north Sligo; they made it to fourteen of them. That evening, a concert was organised in her honour. As soon as Constance arrived, the packed hall rose to its feet, applauding her for over five minutes. After the musical interlude, Constance rose and gave a rendition of the piece she had recited to her regiment on Easter Sunday. When she finished 'it seemed as if the audience would never stop cheering'. She returned to recite a humorous piece called 'A Recruiting Ballad for the British Army'.

On Monday morning, Constance went on a cruise of Lough Gill and, in the afternoon, she met Éamon de Valera, Count Plunkett, Laurence Ginnell, Joe McGuinness and other visitors who had arrived in Sligo on the midday train. That night, she was conferred with the freedom of the borough at Sligo Town Hall, built on the site of a Cromwellian fortress well known to earlier generations of the Gore-Booth family. A group of fifty Sinn Féin men positioned themselves to ensure that there was no more disturbance and 'some parties who were making themselves objectionable were quietly removed.' When the Mayor spoke, he was rushed by a soldier, who was ejected by Volunteers. He recovered to introduce Constance as 'the mother of a new Ireland'.

In reading the address of freedom, the town clerk said they were honouring not just Constance, but also 'a family of which she was the most distinguished member'. Constance, in reply, acknowledged that she had moved far from her origins: 'I became a rebel because the older I grew and the more I thought and the more I used my eyes and the more I went amongst the people of Ireland, and particularly Dublin, the more I realised that nothing could do Ireland only to get rid of England bag and baggage.'

While the Irish Parliamentary Party had made great promises, young men and women were 'drifting away in a great stream out of the country – our fairest, our youngest and cleverest ... Our mills were empty and I saw nothing but cattle and sheep on lands where we should have human beings.'

She was proud to have called James Connolly 'a friend' and to have worked beside him during the 1913 lock-out. She urged her audience to work for Ireland and expressed the hope that Irish independence would be recognised at the peace conference, 'not only on grounds of sympathy but on logical grounds'. In his speech, Éamon de Valera said that the Countess's speech should convince everyone that they were 'neither wild dreamers or red revolutionaries'. Laurence Ginnell described Constance as 'the Joan of Arc of Ireland'.

While in Sligo, she got news that her Irish Citizen Army comrade William Partridge had died; his funeral would take place at Ballaghaderreen, which was within reach of Ballymote. On Tuesday, Constance attended the funeral, wearing her Easter Week tunic. She spoke in Ballymote and, after going to mass the next day, was taken to Keash, where there were sports, and lunch at the priest's house. She spoke to young women about her life and work and showed them the rosary beads given to her by William Partridge, which she wore around her wrist. Later she made a speech to 4,000 people.

Two weeks later, she was in Cork. News came through that William Cosgrave had won the Kilkenny by-election and, as the train travelled south, cheering crowds and bonfires on the hills celebrated another Sinn

Féin victory. Constance was photographed in Kilkenny with Cosgrave, Darrell Figgis, de Valera and Laurence Ginnell; she was dressed in a long, silky coat and was holding a bouquet.

Cork presented Constance with an 'Address from the Remnant of the Irish Republican Brotherhood of Rebel Cork of '65-67 to Countess Markievicz'. She prized this as much as her address from the ITGWU. She gave two speeches that weekend in Cork and another in Clonakilty, took part in several meetings organised by transport workers, Cumann na mBan and the Fianna, and demonstrated on behalf of prisoners arrested under the Defence of the Realm Act.

Her speeches followed a pattern – first she would exhort her audiences to work for any of the several republican societies connected with Sinn Féin. She would then compare the 1916 Rising to Bunker Hill, a lost battle that helped win a war. Victory for Sinn Féin was defined as recognition for Ireland at the peace conference. Any nation whose people rose up and held its capital city for a week was entitled to be represented at such a conference; or so Sinn Féin believed.

The by-election victories for Sinn Féin in North Roscommon, South Longford, East Clare and Kilkenny City were the first fruits of the Rising. A party with no funds, no central organisation and no staff had taken seats from an Irish Parliamentary Party that had powerful local organisations and financial support. For the British administration in Dublin Castle, the new Sinn Féin policy was an affront. It ignored the existence of the Castle administration and treated British law in Ireland as illegal. The administration began making arrests.

By September, fourteen men had been arrested for supporting Sinn Féin's new constitutional movement. They denounced the court, ignored the judges and demanded to be treated as prisoners of war. Among those arrested was Thomas Ashe, charged with sedition for a speech he made in Ballinalee, County Longford, where Michael Collins was also speaking. He was detained at the Curragh and then transferred to Mountjoy Gaol in Dublin to serve two years' hard labour. In Mountjoy, Austin Stack acted as the prisoners' commandant and, with Ashe and others, demanded prisoner of war status. On 18 September, when their demands were refused, they went on hunger strike. On 25 September, Ashe died at the Mater Hospital after being force-fed by prison authorities. Dr Kathleen Lynn, who saw him before he lost consciousness, was sure that food had found its way into his lungs. At the inquest into his death, the jury condemned the staff at the prison for the 'inhuman and dangerous operation performed on the prisoner, and other acts of unfeeling and barbaric conduct'.

Constance wrote to Eva about Ashe's 'heroic' death. She felt that the British were trying to goad republicans into another rising so that they could wipe them all out. On every street were machine guns and armoured cars, manned by 'masses of soldiers'. When she had given a talk in Cork, the British had mobilised a regiment with four machine guns in a neighbouring street.

Ashe's funeral on 30 September was an opportunity for nationalists to show their strength. An advance guard of armed Volunteers, followed by nearly 200 priests, led the procession of 30,000 mourners. Many were armed and wearing the forbidden uniforms of the Volunteers, Cumann na mBan, the Fianna and the Irish Citizen Army. The funeral oration was given by Michael Collins who, until then, was unknown to most. After the last post sounded, three volleys were fired and Collins spoke: 'The volley we have just heard is the only speech it is proper to make above the grave of a dead Fenian'. The British army looked on silently.

On Sunday 21 October, Constance received an overwhelming reception in the small Limerick village of Athea, the home town of Con Colbert, one of her Fianna boys, who had been executed for his part in the Rising. So packed were the streets that one spectator worried that the buildings themselves might collapse under the pressure. Following an open-air meeting in a field, Constance was the guest of honour for lunch in Colbert's home, Gale View.

Ordinary politics had resumed and, at Sinn Féin's tenth annual *ard fheis* on 25–6 October in Dublin's Mansion House, the various strands of the movement came together. Éamon de Valera emerged as the new leader of the revamped organisation when both Arthur Griffith and Count Plunkett graciously withdrew their names. Although the original Sinn Féin abhorred physical violence and had never sought a complete break with Britain, it was decided to hold on to the old name, by now associated with all Irish nationalists. A new constitution was accepted that declared Sinn Féin's intention to deny the right of the British parliament to legislate for Ireland was accepted.

An issue that threatened to split the convention was raised by Constance. Like many, she found Eoin MacNeill's efforts to stop the Easter Rising at the last minute hard to forgive. Pearse, in his final address to his soldiers during Easter week, had struck a conciliatory note. 'Of the fatal countermanding order which prevented those plans from being carried out, I shall not speak further. Both Eoin MacNeill and we have acted in the best interest of Ireland.' De Valera, in prison, had resolved not to let the matter split the Volunteers. When MacNeill arrived with a group of prisoners at Dartmoor, where de Valera was held at the time, he ordered his men to salute MacNeill. If Sinn Féin was to win an election, presenting a united front was vital.

Constance opposed the election of MacNeill to Sinn Féin's 24-member executive on the grounds that he had changed his mind many times. She was supported by Kathleen Clarke and a few others. Clarke, who had told Constance she would not support such a motion, changed her mind when she saw the hostility 'a woman who had come out and risked her life' faced at the meeting. De Valera spoke in MacNeill's defence, pointing out that he had never made any claims to be a revolutionary. MacNeill had retained the respect of the majority and was elected to the executive with 888 votes – more than the 617 received by Constance.

During the discussion on the constitution, the resolution 'that the equality of men and women in this organisation be emphasised in all speeches and leaflets' was introduced, with women determined not to be sidelined. Kathleen Lynn and Jenny Wyse Power stressed the need for talented women as well as men in the new Ireland. The pair were supported by Seán T. O'Kelly and the motion was passed. Kathleen Lynn, Kathleen Clarke and Josephine Countess Plunkett as well as Constance were elected to a new 24-member executive. Jenny Wyse Power was co-opted soon after, replacing Countess Plunkett. These politically active women still faced a wall of indifference if not downright hostility: at the convention, just seventeen of the thousand delegates who attended were women and only Waterford-based Rosamund Jacob came from outside Dublin.

At the Irish Volunteers convention in Croke Park a few weeks later, de Valera was elected president, making him the military as well as the civil leader of Irish republicanism. Cathal Brugha was chief of staff of the Volunteers and his great rival Michael Collins became director of organisation. Collins was an IRB member, as was the Fianna founding member Seán McGarry, who was the general secretary. De Valera had given up his brief IRB membership.

As well as her work with Sinn Féin, Cumann na mBan and the Fianna, Constance was on the committee of the Irish Republican Prisoners Dependants' Fund. She was re-elected president of Cumann na mBan at its 1917 autumn convention and remained chief scout of the Fianna, who made Éamon de Valera their president. With the Fianna, she believed that there was a continuing need for a link with the Volunteers, although – interestingly – she did not fully support the idea that all Irish of military age be trained in the use of arms, believing that this should be an individual decision. In early December she was in Belfast where, a few days after her visit, two Fianna were caught carrying a sackload of bombs that they had smuggled from Scotland.

At the first meeting of the Sinn Féin executive on 19 December 1917, Constance was appointed to head a Department of Labour along with Cathal O'Shannon, who represented the labour movement. No documents of the time explain this decision, although the account of a meeting on 4 March 1918 mentions vaguely that Constance had submitted 'a report' of some kind and that it was accepted.

Although loved by the public, especially in Dublin, Constance was not entirely accepted in nationalist circles. The Sinn Féin Club at Tulla, County Clare, threatened to burn a lookalike model of the 'dreaded' Countess and the superior of the Christian Brothers in Ireland was not amused when he discovered that the Countess was invited to visit CBS Tullamore and speak to the boys. In 1918, Griffith expressed his annoyance at her flamboyant rhetoric and 'idiotic revolutionary speeches'.

Her relationship with the labour movement was also changing. After the Rising, Thomas Johnson, a moderate Home Ruler, became leader of the Labour Party. Constance would never establish the same kind of warm personal relationship with him, or with the ITGWU's William O'Brien, as she had enjoyed with Connolly and Larkin. Party politics were played down in the labour movement after 1916; the ITGWU, whose membership had grown from 5,000 in April 1916 to 68,000 by 1918, concentrated on economic rather than political goals.

She found time, as always, for children, holding a Christmas party for nearly 700 youngsters at Liberty Hall in December 1917. In early 1918 she travelled to Manchester with Cathal O'Shannon to raise funds for the James Connolly Labour College and, in Cork, spoke on the place of international labour in an independent republic. In February, suffragists celebrated their first victory when the vote was given to all women over the age of thirty. In that spring of 1918, the Irish Women's Workers Union was registered as a trade union with Louie Bennett and Helen Chevenix as honorary secretaries; membership by then had risen to 5,000. At the time, women's wages were generally less than a third of a man's average.

In March 1918, John Redmond died from complications following an operation for gallstones. A few weeks later, with no Redmond to hold him back, the British prime minster, Lloyd George, extended the Military Services Bill to Ireland; in effect, he was introducing conscription. Lloyd George saw two good reasons for doing this – it would provide badly needed troops for the war effort and would reduce the numbers tempted to join the republican army. In an attempt to prevent a backlash in Ireland, he linked the move to a new Home Rule bill, so alienating both nationalists and unionists.

Every member of the Irish Parliamentary Party voted against the new bill and, when it was passed, they all walked out of the House of Commons in protest, returning to Ireland to link up with Sinn Féin in organising resistance. Never again would southern Irish MPs sit in the House of Commons. De Valera, after a stirring statement reminding the British of the unselfish heroism of Irishmen in Flanders, Suvla Bay, Gallipoli, Egypt, Arabia, Mesopotamia, Mons and Ypres, persuaded the Irish Catholic bishops, then meeting in Maynooth, to denounce the bill.

After a conference in Dublin's Mansion House on 18 April held by Lord Mayor Laurence O'Neill, an Irish Anti-Conscription Committee was convened, representing all shades of political opinion. An anti-conscription pledge was read out at masses all over the country on Sunday 21 April. In all, two million men and women signed a declaration to resist any effort to force Irish men into the British army. Constance joined other leaders in an anti-conscription campaign that brought the Irish Women's Franchise League, Cumann na mBan and other women's organisations together to express their opposition. De Valera came up with an anti-conscription pledge: 'Denying the right of the British Government to enforce compulsory service in this country, we pledge ourselves solemnly to one another to resist conscription by the most effective means at our disposal.'

On 23 April, nearly the whole of Ireland (Belfast excepted) took part in a one-day strike organised with the approval of the Irish Labour Congress. Esther Roper's brother, Reginald, came to Dublin as an observer and met Constance. Machine guns were placed on the Bank of Ireland building on Dublin's College Green in anticipation of another rising. The British, with its army desperate for men, were determined to enforce the bill. Field Marshal Lord French, the newly appointed viceroy, took a hard-line view: 'If they do not come, we will fetch them'. His sister, the militant feminist Charlotte Despard, was one of thousands to oppose him. After a mass meeting at the Mansion House, a national women's day was organised, while women all over the country pledged not to take over jobs left open by men if they were conscripted.

With fury mounting among all sections of Irish society, Edward Shortt, the newly appointed Chief Secretary for Ireland, came up with a plan to arrest all known activists and to put extra troops on standby. To provide a reason, Dublin Castle concocted with a risible tale of 'treasonable communication with the German enemy' after Joseph Dowling, a former member of Roger Casement's Irish brigade, was arrested when he came ashore from a U-boat off the Galway coast allegedly with a message for Sinn Féin from German leaders. On the night of 17/18 May, seventy-three prominent members of Sinn Féin were arrested and deported immediately.

Constance, whose many 'seditious' speeches had been noted by the authorities, was among them. She had left the Sinn Féin headquarters on Harcourt Street, walked to Maud Gonne MacBride's house on nearby St Stephen's Green and then set off for Rathmines where she was living at the time with the Ginnells. Near the entrance to Portobello Barracks, she was stopped by six soldiers and two detectives and told to get into an armoured car. Her brown cocker spaniel, Poppet, jumped in with her. She was taken first to Dublin Castle and then to Kingstown early the next morning, along with the others who had been arrested. Among them were Maud Gonne MacBride, Kathleen Clarke, Arthur Griffith, Count Plunkett, Éamon de Valera and William Cosgrave.

After they were loaded into the hold of a gunboat, they crossed the Irish Sea in the mid-afternoon, arriving in Holyhead at 10pm. The following day, the men were taken to Usk and Gloucester jails, while Constance was kept in the Holyhead police station and then brought to London by train. On her way, she was asked to pay six shillings for her dog's ticket.

At Euston, she found Eva waiting. While travelling, Constance had experienced a strong urge to see her sister, regretting that she had not had time to tell her of her arrest. In London, Esther Roper felt a pressing urge to go to Euston and meet the Irish mail train. With Eva in tow, she set off for the station and, when they arrived, they split up to search the platform. Soon after, Roper spied 'the strangest little procession' coming towards her. It was led by a brown cocker spaniel, followed by a couple of soldiers with rifles, then Eva and Constance and finally an officer with a drawn sword.

A detective opened the door of a taxi and Constance got in accompanied by an escort; Poppet jumped in too. Eva heard the detective tell the driver to go to Holloway Prison. A few hours later, Poppet was brought to Eva's flat; he was later sent back to Ireland where he stayed with the Bartons in Glendalough, County Wicklow, until Constance returned. Robert Barton, an officer with the Royal Dublin Fusiliers during the 1916 Rising, resigned his commission in disgust at the heavy-handed British treatment of the rebels and joined the republican cause, as did his cousin Erskine Childers. Barton became Sinn Féin member for West Wicklow in 1918. His sister Dulcibella was a good friend of Constance's.

Joining Constance in Holloway were Maud Gonne MacBride and Kathleen Clarke. The three women were given cells after the 'Hard Nails Wing' of the prison was emptied. Between their cells were three empty ones. In each cell was a camp bed with slats and a mattress that seemed to be made of hay according to Kathleen Clarke; the hills and hollows that developed, along with the board-hard pillows and coarse blankets and sheets made sleep difficult, although Constance made no complaint, cheerfully maintaining that she could sleep on stones. The three women were given just one hour a day for exercise. For the remaining twenty-three hours, they were locked up.

As internees, the women were allowed to have food, clothes, books and approved newspapers sent in. Early on, Kathleen Clarke remembered asking Constance whether she was paying to have her meals sent in; Constance confessed that she was doing so because she was recovering from a bout of measles. The arrests were good propaganda for Ireland. On 23 June, Arthur Griffith, then held in Reading jail, won a by-election in East Cavan, beating the Irish Parliamentary Party's candidate. Constance was elated. 'Such a victory, our arrests did it ... Putting us away cleared the issues for us so much better than our own speeches ever could.'

She was growing increasingly sceptical about the value of leaders, who could be 'such a curse' since power so often got 'into the hands of a clique'. She shared her distaste for parliamentary politics with many Irish activists, believing that the national revolution would be in vain if the existing structures were left intact. As a supporter of the co-operative movement, she believed that, with their leaders in prison, people would be forced to think for themselves.

The practical joker in Constance was never far from the surface. She had her fun with the censor who read her letters, writing that she was probably accused of taking part in the 'German Plot' because of the German measles she had contracted just before she was arrested. Her first few to Eva were signed *Auf Wiedersehn*.

As the most experienced of the three 'jailbirds', Constance worried about her companions. When Maud Gonne MacBride was arrested, her son Seán had despairingly run after the Black Maria that was taking her away. In Holloway, she was not allowed to sign a cheque to provide for him. Kathleen Clarke, after the horror of losing both husband and brother during the Rising, worried about her three children. She found the prison diet of cocoa, margarine and 'a thing they called skilly' repulsive. When she became alarmingly thin, the doctor put her – and MacBride – on a 'hospital' diet that included tea, rice pudding and milk. Constance persuaded the doctor to allow them two hours of exercise and fresh air every day; later, they were permitted as much time as they liked out of doors. Under this regime, Constance's health improved and she stopped having her meals sent in.

Kathleen Clarke continued to fight for a better diet and persuaded the doctor to give them an egg each a day. When she continued to lose weight, she refused a move to the hospital, as the doctor wished, unless places were also found for her friends, even though Constance's fussing exasperated her. 'I told her one day that if she wanted an occupation to look elsewhere, that I was in no humour to provide her with an occupation or thrills, but that did not choke her off', she wrote in her autobiography. In the end, the doctor found beds for all three in the hospital.

A consequence of moving to the hospital was that the women were allowed visitors. First to arrive on 27 August was Eva Gore-Booth. 'Madame came back from her sister's visit in a wild state of excitement, bringing a large basket of fruit and flowers', reported Clarke. After a warning not to speak of politics, their conversation was witnessed and noted by a prison observer. Constance elaborated on her arrest and trip to Holloway, claiming that Poppet, her dog, was taught to 'strafe' anything English on the journey. She asked where the dog was now, wondered whether Eva had received a cheque for £20 (she hadn't) and put in a request for sketching materials. She wondered why the male prisoners got larger sheets of writing paper than the women and why her post was held up.

Maud Gonne MacBride had a visit from her son Seán and daughter Iseult, while Kathleen Clarke's sisters were to travel from Limerick. A few weeks later, a report in the *Irish Independent* described the conditions enforced for the visits. These, Clarke felt, 'were designed to humiliate us and our visitors', and so she cancelled her request to see her sisters. Constance agreed with Mrs Clarke; MacBride did not.

The author Patricia Lynch was a frequent caller at Holloway, leaving food, flowers, books and other treats. Knowing that both Constance and MacBride were keen gardeners, friends sent them potted plants. When these wilted in the dank cells, the pair left them in the exercise yard on alternate nights to help them grow. To brighten up the grey ugliness of their 'cage', they decorated their cells with bunches of grapes, ribbons and coloured clothes.

In the early days, Clarke heard MacBride and Constance arguing about their respective social status. Constance claimed that she had belonged to the inner circle of the vice-regal set, while MacBride was 'only on the fringes of it'. The women would then complain about each other to Clarke. She found it quite a strain, although she came to like both her companions. Clarke felt that Constance patronised her, wondering why such 'an insignificant person as myself' was put in prison with her. Her attitude was that the British were a 'blundering lot of fools to arrest someone like me'.

Throughout 1918, the arrests and the restrictions did little to improve the state of chaotic anarchy in Ireland. All nationalist organisations were proscribed, including the GAA, since a crowd could assemble easily at a football or hurling match. In defiance of the ban, 1,500 hurling matches were held on 4 August while, on 15 August, nearly 2,000 Sinn Féin meetings were held in one hour. By August, Sinn Féin had 81,000 members in 1,025 clubs, each with a company of Volunteers. In that month, Hanna Sheehy Skeffington, arrested outside the offices of the Irish Women's Franchise League after her visit to the USA, spent one day in Holloway. Constance had not seen her since Easter week.

In October, to the great relief of Constance and Kathleen, Maud Gonne MacBride was sent to a nursing home in London. She had become morose and depressed while in jail. Clarke was told that she could be released on similar grounds if she appealed to the British government; she said she would never appeal to the British government for anything. The remaining pair were given a gas ring and Constance took to making stews; Kathleen became the practical joker, on one occasion giving Constance soap to flavour the stew. When she was offered whiskey as a stimulant, she passed it on to Constance, who, unlike her, was not a teetotaller.

On 9 November, May Power wrote to Constance to tell her that a boy had won first prize in an essay competition conducted by the *Catholic Bulletin* on the subject of 'My Favourite Heroine'. His essay was just one of many written about Constance.

The long and bloody world war ended on 11 November 1918. From 21 November, when the Parliament (Qualification of Women) Act 1918 came into force, women over thirty were not only allowed to vote but could stand for election to parliament for the first time. This had the effect of tripling the British electorate from 7.7 million in 1912 to 21.4 million by the end of 1918. Women now accounted for about 43 per cent of the electorate and, had those over twenty-one been enfranchised, women would have outnumbered men. When an election was called for 14 December, Sinn Féin asked Constance to stand. It would be the first general election in the United Kingdom since December 1910. She agreed, for 'sport'.

The opening meeting of the Sinn Féin campaign was held on 11 November with jubilant Armistice Day celebrations as a backdrop.

Sinn Féin would put up candidates in all the existing constituencies. Of the seventy-three Sinn Féin candidates, forty-even were in jail – better propaganda than any number of speeches, as Constance noted: 'Sending you to jail is like pulling out all the loud stops on all the speeches you ever made or words you ever wrote!'

Constance was standing in Dublin's St Patrick's Division, one of the four Dublin constituencies at that time. It consisted of the Merchant's Quay, Usher's Quay and Wood Quay inner-city wards. The Irish Women's Franchise League and Cumann na mBan did most of the hard work on the ground, although Sinn Féin did hold a rally on her behalf. She managed to send out an election address, dated 11 November:

> It is with great pleasure that I have been accepted as SF candidate for St Patrick's constituency. As I will not procure my freedom by giving any pledge or undertaking to the enemy, you will probably have to fight without me. I have many friends in the constituency who will work all the harder for me. They know that I stand for the Irish Republic, to establish which our heroes died, and that my colleagues are firm in the belief that the freeing of Ireland is in the hands of the Irish people today ... There are many roads to freedom. Today we may hope that our road to freedom will be a peaceful and bloodless one; I need hardly assure you that it will be an honourable one. I would never take an oath of allegiance to the power that I meant to overthrow ... The one thing to bear in mind is that this election must voice the people of Ireland's demand to be heard at the peace conference ... We are quite cheerful and ready for anything that comes.

She sent a note from Holloway urging co-operation between Sinn Féin and the Irish trade union movement. Since the first principle of Sinn Féin was to end the connection with England, 'Sinn Féiners affiliated or amalgamated with English trade unions should be recommended when possible to sever the English connections'. She also believed that they should make it their business to secure a living wage for workers.

Constance also wrote to the Irish Women's Franchise League: 'One reason I'd like to win is that we could make St Patrick's a rallying ground for women and a splendid centre for constructive work by women. I am full of schemes and ideas'. In the election address sent to the Sinn Féin director of elections in Dublin, she wrote that she stood for a republic such as Connolly 'wrote about, worked for and died for'.

> Real democratic control with economic and industrial as well as political freedom. To organise our new nation on just and equitable lines, avoiding the mistakes other Nations have made in allowing the powers of Government, law, force, education, foreign policy, etc, to be the birthright of the moneyed classes to be used by them for the further accumulation of wealth and the building up of a class tyranny daily more subtle and more difficult to seize and overthrow.

Women, she argued, must 'trust women to speak for them, to work for them and fight for them and to look after their interests in the Irish Republic'.

Because the winter was bitterly cold, Kathleen Clarke spent much of the day in bed and, to keep herself busy, requested material for knitting, crochet, lace-making and embroidery. Inspired by her friend, Constance acquired materials for sketching and painting and many of the watercolours she painted in Holloway have survived. She painted remembered scenes of Ireland and heroic figures from the past. She tried her hand at an illumination on the topic of Connolly's 'The Cause of Labour is the Cause of Ireland'. Among the pictures was a caricature of Kathleen trying to thread a needle with her face all puckered up. Clarke liked it: 'It really was very funny, and very clever.'

Constance had a habit of smoking when she came into Kathleen's room, which had a gate to it rather than a door. She would drop cigarette ash and flick the paint and water off her brush. Because Kathleen liked order and Constance's untidiness 'distracted' her, she told her to leave the room. Constance sat in the corridor, heaving deep sighs. Next morning she asked very meekly if she could come in. 'No', said Kathleen, 'I have had enough of you'. Constance tried again, promising to bring a plate for her cigarette ash and a jar for her paint brush. Still Kathleen would not relent. 'But Kathleen, I'm lonely', said Constance. Kathleen gave in.

The pair tried to make their humdrum life as pleasant as possible and such quarrels were rare. Constance stole the wardress's report book in which was noted every move either of them made and they had much fun reading it. Reading helped pass the time, with Constance favouring poetry, especially Robert Browning. She also ordered books on economics, labour, socialism and history from the library and flicked her way through them. 'She would skim through a book, trying in her quick way to get the sense of it,' said Clarke.

On 14 December, Irish women marched to the polling booths for the first time, led by ninety-year-old Anna Haslam, who, with her late husband, Thomas, had founded the Dublin Suffrage Society in 1874. The issue was clear: a vote for Sinn Féin was a vote for a free and independent Irish republic. By a majority of 70 per cent, the Irish people voted for Sinn Féin. The Irish Parliamentary Party dropped from eighty seats at the beginning of the year to a paltry seven. Their fight for Home Rule was over.

One Sunday morning in December, Constance had a visit from the governor and the matron, bringing the news that she had been elected a Member of Parliament – the only one of the seventeen women candidates to make it. Among others who stood were Winifred Carney in Belfast and Charlotte Despard in London. 'Madame got so excited she went yelling and dancing all over the place,' said Clarke. In the St Patrick's Division, Constance polled 7,835 votes; William Field of the Irish Parliamentary Party, who had held the seat for twenty-six years, got 3,741 and Alderman J.J. Kelly won 312 votes.

Outside the Sinn Féin headquarters on Dublin's Harcourt Street, an excited crowd had watched as the figures from the counting centres were displayed on a giant noticeboard in a second-floor window. That Sinn Féin could win by such a huge margin was the stuff of dreams. 'The humbug was now over,' as Joseph Cleary said when speaking on behalf of a triumphant Markievicz. Not everyone was pleased with her election. A leader in the *Irish Independent* questioned her 'mental balance'; this 'mean and unjustified attack' provoked angry letters to the paper from Maud Gonne MacBride and Jenny Wyse Power.

On Christmas Day, after Constance decorated the small passage outside the Holloway cells with flowers, she and Kathleen had a 'grand dinner' with food sent by Clarke's sisters in Limerick, and a bottle of champagne from Eva. Soon after, Kathleen became ill with heart trouble, possibly connected to the flu epidemic then raging. Not wanting another

Irish martyr, on 19 February the authorities decided to release her and she stayed with Eva until she was fit enough to return home. Constance remained in Holloway for a further three weeks: 'Of course, I miss K very much, though for the first time in my life, I was thankful to see the back of a dear friend.' In an affectionate letter, she sent Kathleen 'heaps of love' and wondered 'whose head you are snapping off now.'

She was hungry for news of Ireland and worried about her husband who 'hated wars, revolutions and politics' and of whom she had heard nothing since 1916. She knew indirectly that her stepson, attached to the Russian Volunteer Fleet at Archangel as an interpreter, was still alive. 'Poor Staskou, I'd hate him to be killed or wounded; he did love life so.'

From Holloway, she wrote a letter to the young playwright Frank J. Hugh O'Donnell, about his play *The Dawn Mist*. Praising his ability to write about 'the idealism and spirit of self-sacrifice that is the keynote of the true Irish character', she takes a cut at depictions of stage Irishry 'merely picturesque results of our history' and signs off in Irish – *Mise ar gCúis na hÉireann* (Yours in the cause of Ireland). The letter was used as a foreword to the printed edition of the play.

No one watching the elections could doubt that the Irish wanted to rule themselves. On 7 January 1919, twenty-six of the elected Sinn Féin members met at Dublin's Mansion House to make plans for convening an Irish parliament three weeks later.

CHAPTER FOURTEEN

Nineteen Hundred and Nineteen

On Tuesday, 21 January 1919, the first Dáil Éireann met in the Round Room of Dublin's Mansion House, watched closely by the press and many international visitors; long queues had formed on the street outside. Dublin Castle had decided to ignore the Dáil; the viceroy, Lord French, thought the occasion so ludicrous that he had withdrawn the need for a police permit.

Presiding was Cathal Brugha, since both the president (de Valera) and vice-president (Arthur Griffith) were in jail. Members were called *Teachta Dáil* – the Irish for deputies of parliament; the word *Dáil* meant 'assembly'. By an extraordinary coincidence, as the new members of parliament walked into the Mansion House at around 3.30pm, members of the Royal Fusiliers were departing after a celebration lunch.

A prayer from the 'Rebel Priest', Father Michael O'Flanagan, opened the ceremony, which was conducted mainly in Irish, to the bemusement of the visiting press but also to many locals, few of them fluent Irish speakers. Only twenty-four members were present with a further thirty-five described as *Fe ghlas ag Gallaibh* or 'In a foreign prison'. All were Sinn Féin members and most were young, urban, middle-class men, with Constance, a 51-year-old woman, the notable exception. Unionists had declined the invitation to join the new assembly.

Among the documents hastily prepared for the occasion was a 'Democratic Programme' based on the 1916 Proclamation, with the labour leader Tom Johnson its main architect. Its radical programme might have been a ploy to influence the International

Socialist Conference taking place in Bern, Switzerland; the 'Second International', formed in 1889 and dissolved in 1916, had supported the demands of Irish republicans, as had Russia. An Irish Declaration of Independence was read, firstly in French and then in English, followed by a 'Message to the Free Nations of the World' in French and English aimed squarely at the Versailles Peace Conference then meeting in France. Under a provisional constitution, the Dáil gave itself full powers of legislation and absolute control over finance. With the business of the day complete by 5.20pm, a celebratory dinner followed.

In the wider world, the Red Army had occupied Sebastopol in the Crimea as the Bolshevik effort to drive the Allies out of Russia continued. There were fears that Bolshevism could sweep through the continent of Europe. Farther afield, Britain faced revolts in Egypt, Afghanistan and India.

In the early months of 1919, the Catholic Church had warned of links between Bolshevism and Sinn Féin, and Bishop Kelly of Rosse criticised the leaders of the Dáil, especially Constance, for their extremist tendencies. Constance declared to a Sinn Féin meeting that if President Wilson failed to support Ireland, they should turn to the Bolsheviks, who had consistently supported the Irish cause. Republicans at the time were friendly towards the Bolsheviks and news of Bolshevik atrocities and barbarity was received with suspicion. With Woodrow Wilson, in Constance's view, 'a dark horse' likely to lose sight of Ireland's cause, she suspected that the League of Nations might not favour small nations after all, leaving them open to other alliances.

Through Nora Connolly, Constance had 'first-hand news' of the industrial advances in Russia but she heard also of terrible ruthlessness towards perceived enemies of the Republic, including 'cruel and drastic' executions.

She disliked autocracy of any kind but was optimistic:

> ... surely if they have the sense to organise education, they can abolish class. While they are menaced by the moneyed classes of the whole world, their only hope lies in the success of a strong central government: a tyranny in fact, but once the pressure is relieved, Lenin survives, and he has not lost his original ideals. We may hope. Of course, they may go mad with the idea of Empire,

and go out with their armies to force the world to come under their ideas and do awful things in the name of freedom, small nationalities, etc, but even so they have done something.

She believed that the Bolshevik revolution was the natural successor to the French revolution. Both had overthrown undemocratic autocracies and attempted to build new societies based on equality for all. To see violence as justified and necessary in order to discard a discredited regime was part of the prevailing tradition of romantic nationalism. Later, Constance would admit that she knew little of the Bolsheviks but, at the time, she argued that they were akin to the ancient Irish in their commitment to 'decentralisation' through 'soviets' or local councils.

The first task of the new assembly was to press the case for Irish independence at the Versailles Peace Conference that had started on 18 January and would continue for a year. As far as republicans were concerned, they had fulfilled the conditions for nationhood set down by President Wilson in his 4 July 1918 speech: 'What we seek is a reign of law based on the consent of the governed and sustained by the organised opinion of mankind.' Éamon de Valera, Arthur Griffith and Count Plunkett were nominated as delegates by the new Dáil and Seán T. O'Kelly set off for Paris to secure their admission to the conference. In March, he was joined by George Gavan Duffy. In the USA, friends of the Irish cause persuaded Congress to pass a resolution asking that Ireland be admitted to the peace conference.

In the early months of the year, appeals and protests about the continued imprisonment of Constance and the other Irish internees went unheeded. Invitations from the prime minister, Lloyd George, in 10 Downing Street, hoping that 'it might be convenient for the newly elected MPs to attend the opening of the new parliament on 11 February', were forwarded to the Irish MPs in their jails in England. Constance received hers a week after parliament opened and she enjoyed composing a suitably acerbic reply, though she suspected it never went further than the prison censor. She was continuing her studies of political systems, going through the works of H.N. Brailsford, a man who fought against secret 'diplomacy', and the hard-line Bolshevik Maxim Litvinov who, like Connolly, argued that power must lie in the hands of the working class.

England was in the grip of the worst flu epidemic in its history and one of its victims was Pierce McCann, an Irish internee held in Gloucester jail. Aware that they might be creating a new set of Irish martyrs, the British decided to release the remaining Irish internees. Constance left Holloway on 10 March and spent a few days with Eva and Esther in London before returning to Ireland. Eva had organised meetings with British trade union leaders and socialist activists for her sister. Constance could not resist a visit to Westminster, where she dropped into the members' vestibule and was amused to see that the place reserved for her coat and hat in the cloakroom was next to that of Sir Edward Carson. Many thought her refusal to take her seat a missed opportunity for women. It would be another few months before Lady Astor, elected the Conservative MP for Plymouth after her husband was elevated to the Lords, would become the first woman MP to sit in the venerable chamber of the House of Commons.

When Constance returned to Dublin, arriving by the 6pm mail boat at Kingstown on Saturday 15 March, she received an even more jubilant reception than twenty-one months earlier following her release from Aylesbury.

> Madame O'Rahilly and Mrs Humphries met me at Holyhead, and they had secured sunny seats on the boat. The sun on the rippling sea was divine, and the seagulls gave the finishing touch to the reality of freedom. I was met by deputations of everybody! We motored in to Dublin to Liberty Hall. Last time was nothing to it. The crowd had no beginning or end. I made a speech, and then we formed up in a torchlight procession and went to St Patrick's. Every window had a flag or candles or both. You never saw such excitement.

Police were under orders from the Under-Secretary not to interfere. As an elected member of parliament, this was Constance's first opportunity to address her constituents and she had a right to do so. Furthermore, the reception of released prisoners so far had 'fallen very flat', said the chief secretary Edward Shortt, mainly because of the Castle's policy of ignoring them.

One of her first visits was to Kathleen Clarke, who had spent seven weeks in a Dublin nursing home after her return from London and had then gone to stay with her sisters in Limerick. Four rooms at the Clarke household on Richmond Avenue were filled with Markievicz's furniture. At the time of her arrest, Constance was living with the Ginnells, and had brought her furniture and valuable paintings with her. When the Ginnells were forced to move, Kathleen Clarke offered Constance the use of her house while she recuperated from her illness. After Clarke returned from Limerick, Constance asked to stay on and Clarke agreed: 'Though we quarrelled occasionally, I was fond of her; she had some very fine qualities.'

Éamon de Valera had not waited to be released. In February, with the help of Michael Collins, Harry Boland and the wax impression of a key, he had escaped from Lincoln Prison along with two other prisoners. He remained in hiding until the release of all the Irish prisoners was announced. Plans were made for him to return to Dublin on 26 March, where he would be greeted by the Lord Mayor of Dublin in a manner befitting the official head of state. Dublin Castle had no intention of either endorsing the new republic or acknowledging de Valera's status, and the streets of Dublin rumbled to the sound of tanks and armoured cars. The first aeroplanes flew over the city. Fearing bloodshed, de Valera cancelled his reception.

When the Dáil met for its second session on 1 April 1919, fifty-two members were present, including Constance. De Valera was elected president and formed a cabinet. Constance was appointed Secretary for Labour, making her the first official female cabinet minister in western Europe (Alexandra Kollontai had been appointed People's Commissar for Social Welfare in Soviet Russia). Her brief included social welfare. She told Kathleen Clarke that she had threatened to quit Sinn Féin and join the Labour Party if they did not give her the job. Since she had headed the Sinn Féin labour committee in 1917, she felt that she had earned the right to be minister.

Others appointed as ministers were Arthur Griffith (home affairs), Cathal Brugha (defence), Count Plunkett (foreign affairs), Eoin MacNeill (industries), Michael Collins (finance) and William Cosgrave (local government). The Dáil continued to meet, though sporadically, holding six meetings in 1919 and three each in 1920 and 1921. To raise the money it needed to finance its activities, a National Loan was launched at home and in the USA by Michael Collins as Minister for Finance. Although conducting ordinary parliamentary business was difficult, the Dáil was successful in taking control of local government and the court system.

Constance was delighted with her new position and wrote to her sister on notepaper headed 'Dáil Éireann, Department of Labour, Mansion House'. 'It is so funny, suddenly, to be a Government and supposed to be respectable!' Her first job as Minister concerned the plight of two child prisoners-of-war. On 21 January, while the first Dáil was meeting in Dublin, Dan Breen, Séumas Robinson, Seán Hogan, Seán Treacy and at least five others had provided a stark reminder that the gunmen were very much prepared to fight on. In an ambush on South Tipperary County Council, employees carrying explosives to Solobeaghead quarry and their armed Royal Irish Constabulary (RIC) escort, Constables Patrick McDonnell and James O'Connell, were killed, provoking widespread criticism, even within Sinn Féin. During its investigation, the RIC seized an eight-year-old boy, John Connor, and questioned him for over four hours. Along with his fifteen-year-old brother Matthew and eleven-year-old-friend Timothy Connors, he was held for ten weeks.

When questioned in the House of Commons, the Attorney General for Ireland, A.W. Samuels, replied that the children were not arrested, but rather 'removed from the neighbourhood' to ensure their 'personal safety'. Constance's committee reported the safe release of the boys, as well as of other republican prisoners.

In August 1919, the Dáil founded a National Conciliation Board for the settlement of trade disputes that came under Constance and the Department of Labour. In one of the first industrial disputes involving her ministry, the Irish Transport and General Workers' Union was negotiating with a Dublin manufacturer of beads who was underpaying his employees. The meeting at the Sinn Féin offices in Harcourt Street was dragging on, with no apparent hope of settlement. Constance thought up a ruse to hurry matters along. She rushed into the meeting room with the urgent news that the military were on their way in fifteen minutes. Still neither side would give an inch. Five minutes later, she told them that they had only ten minutes left. Neither side listened. Only when she warned the meeting that the military would arrive in just five minutes did the employer sign an agreement.

Seán O'Faoláin maintained that Constance was received with scant courtesy by her fellow Dáil members between August 1921 and June

1922. Her memoranda were shuffled from one meeting to another and often ignored. Collins, who funded the various departments, had described the Department of Labour as 'a bloody joke' with little to do. Labour got the smallest allocation of funds of any ministry and Constance did not demand more. In 1920, it was allocated £450; later Constance got a further £500 for the Labour Arbitration Tribunal. By comparison, the Irish language department got £5,000 and propaganda received £900. Yet Constance, although she was on the run, worked hard, setting up conciliation boards and arbitrating disputes, while her department issued guidelines on wages and food prices. The problem was a general lack of interest in labour matters.

Following her second spell in prison, Constance embarked on a whirlwind programme of Dáil meetings, committee meetings and meetings with workers and employers all over the country and occasionally abroad. Much of her work was conducted in secret; there were no limousines, plush offices or lengthy lunches for the new cabinet ministers, although they were paid an annual salary. Constance insisted that deputies' expenses be monitored closely, that public funds should cover only a third-class rail ticket and that the per diem maintenance allowance be no more than fifteen shillings.

At the end of April, Constance was in Glasgow, addressing a huge meeting; on 11 May, she presided at the Fianna *Aeridheacht*, an open-air gathering. The following weekend, she was in Cork attending meetings. She had been invited to attend a *Feis Mór* in Newmarket by the local branch of the Gaelic League and, after arriving late on Saturday evening, she gave a brief speech. 'Boycott English manufacturers and burn everything English except their coal,' she said, quoting Jonathan Swift. After the meeting, her short journey to the Railway Hotel was observed closely by the local police. When they saw a woman who looked like Constance leaving the hotel, they followed her to the local train station where they saw her take a train out of town. What they did not realise was that the woman they had seen off was Madge McCarthy, who acted as a decoy while Constance slipped away from the hotel, spending the night at the Corney Lenihan home in Drom an Airgil. On Sunday morning, Constance sat on the platform for the *Feis Mór*, with only a few policemen in evidence.

The following week, Constance revisited Glasgow before returning to Dublin to meet the three members of the American Commission on

Irish Independence. Edward F. Dunne, a former governor of Illinois, Frank P. Walsh from New York and Michael J. Ryan of Philadelphia had come to Ireland from Paris at the invitation of de Valera and with the approval of the British. They spent a month touring the country and their report, issued in June 1919, was sent to British government officials, to newspapers and to American delegates attending the Versailles peace talks. It formed part of the official USA government publication on the treaty talks.

At Holyhead, the Americans were shocked by the number of armed British soldiers waiting for the ferry to Kingstown. At the time, Ireland was occupied by over 100,000 men, equipped with lorries, armoured cars, tanks, machine guns, artillery and bomber planes. In addition, 15,000 RIC policemen – whom the Americans described as belonging to a branch of the military – lived in barracks and were armed with rifles as well as side arms.

Despite initial opposition from the governor, the American trio visited Mountjoy Gaol, where they discovered that only twelve of the prisoners were non-political. They experienced first-hand the restrictions on movement around the country and witnessed numerous assaults on republican men and women on public streets. On 9 May, the Americans attended a special session of Dáil Éireann. Afterwards, on their way to a Mansion House reception, they were stopped by the military, and de Valera was not allowed to pass. Later, the Americans witnessed soldiers brutally assaulting Eoin MacNeill.

The influence of Constance was apparent in the Americans' descriptions of attacks on women and children taken in for interrogation by the police. She had supplied information on education, infant mortality rates, the organisation of labour and the appalling destitution and hunger suffered by many. The Americans had met labour leaders and were impressed:

> Ireland has the best organised and most coherent labour movement in the world. It is being thwarted and suppressed by the army and constabulary. Wages of unskilled workers are below a line which means to them hunger, cold and privation. The wage of skilled labour is far below the minimum for decent existence.

They noted that many Irish labour leaders believed that, unless they were freed from foreign control and exploitation, they would follow the example of the Russians, setting up 'soviets' or workers' governments and refusing to produce wealth for their oppressors.

The Americans' report, signed on 3 June 1919, recommended that the peace conference appoint an impartial committee to investigate the Irish situation: 'today – the darkest of the dark spots on the map'. President Wilson, wary of alienating his British ally, was not prepared to accept their recommendations. If anything, the work of the committee hardened his heart against the Irish cause and parts of the report were used as an excuse to deny safe conduct to Paris for the three Irish delegates. President Wilson's priority at the Versailles conference was setting up a League of Nations, which, he argued, would help smaller nations like Ireland in the future. For this he needed British support and, in June, he announced that the United States, Britain, France and Germany would have a veto on who was admitted to the conference. Sinn Féin had badly misunderstood the purpose of such conferences, which was to decide the fate of the defeated nations and the countries they had annexed. Had the Germans invaded Ireland, then the Irish would have been welcomed unreservedly. Privately, Constance described the League of Nations as 'pompous rubbish (for the benefit of democracy I suppose) about the reduction of armaments when all they wanted was information on their neighbours so they could get one up on them'.

In mid-May, while the Americans were in Ireland, the British suffragist and socialist Sylvia Pankhurst had visited Dublin, speaking at the Trades Hall in Capel Street on 'Russia Today', with Constance chairing the meeting. She had never met Pankhurst before and was impressed. A week later, a messenger from Michael Collins arrived at the Clarke household on Richmond Avenue in Fairview with a warning for Constance to clear out; a raid was expected. She got dressed and hurried to Margaret Skinnider's house on nearby Waverly Avenue, forgetting her glasses; she was forced to call out Margaret's name several times before she found the correct house. She stayed at Waverly Avenue for some months, disguising herself when she went out, most often as an old lady.

On 5 June, the Socialist Party of Ireland planned a Connolly Birthday Concert at the Mansion House. Shortly before it was due to begin, the police drew a cordon across Dawson Street to stop people attending. Near St Stephen's Green, four police and two civilians were injured after an exchange of gunfire. Fearing that this might happen, the Trades Hall in Capel Street had been booked as an alternative venue and here Constance presided over an evening of speeches, music and appeals for funds.

Ten days later, on 15 June, Constance was arrested for the speech she had made in Newmarket four weeks earlier. She was taken to Mallow by special train, accompanied by thirty soldiers and an equal number of police 'armed to the teeth'; it was a 'Gilbertian' comic-opera journey according to a letter she wrote to Hanna Sheehy Skeffington. The American delegates accused the British of arresting her because of the help she had given them. The British denied this, claiming that, in her speech, she had urged people to regard the children of the police as spies, to ostracise them, treat them as lepers, and refuse to sit near them in church or school.

During her trial, she refused to recognise the court and called no witness in her defence. She wished only to deny the charges. Firstly, she would never have advocated the persecution of policemen's children, and, secondly, she had not urged shops to boycott the police because it would be impossible to do so and would achieve nothing.

When she was sentenced to four months in jail, she stood up. 'Three cheers for the Irish Republic,' she cried. The crowd continued to cheer while she was escorted from the building. The authorities had planned to have her moved to Mountjoy Gaol in Dublin, but the governor feared she would escape and so requested a 'strong guard' outside the female prison 'day and night'. The RIC pointed out that employing four shifts of twenty policemen for this purpose would be 'to the very serious detriment' of the city. The proper place to guard prisoners was inside the prison walls.

A suggestion that Constance be moved out of the country was dismissed on the grounds that she had been tried in Ireland. By 10 July, the move to Mountjoy was still under discussion and two large motor lorries, one small lorry and a supplementary escort of twenty military were held in readiness. It was then decided to defer the move until after the peace celebrations, since it was 'not improbable' that Sinn Féin would try to seize her. By 28 July, given her good conduct, it was decided to leave her in Cork.

She 'seemed in good health and contented' when visited by a medical officer of the General Prison Board. Her cell was bright and airy and the exercise ground 'spacious, neat and orderly'. She was well aware of the propaganda value of her detention: 'As long as the jails are full, that keeps the heart in the people – Ireland always hatches a plentiful supply of Phoenix eggs – and of dragon's teeth not a few!'

Her stretch in Cork was not too onerous. She was allowed visitors; friends sent in food and she had all the reading and writing material she wanted. She made a rock garden for the governor and studied history and economics – most notably John Mitchel's *Jail Journal*, which argued that Young Ireland had failed because it could not frame a coherent policy. There was no evidence that her letters were censored. 'This is the most comfortable jail I have been in yet. There's a nice garden, full of pinks, and you can hear the birds sing,' she wrote to Eva. Nora Connolly visited a few times and noted the number of young soldiers employed to guard one woman. She observed that, with no-one to talk to, a sociable woman like Constance must be lonely.

In September, Constance was delighted to get word through Eva of Staskou. She had heard no news of him since he had left Dublin in June 1915 to visit his father. Nor had she heard anything of her husband. He had been in Kiev, which was 'rather a bad place just now' and, with his love of 'fine ideas', he might 'just as easily be a Bolshevik as anything else'. She remembered that, in Dublin, Casimir could lunch with the enemy and sup with the enemy and 'between the two make a wild rebel speech'. She had not written to either her stepson or husband, afraid they might be put on a 'black list' by corresponding with 'a rebel like me'.

That September, while Constance was still in jail, the Dáil and Sinn Féin were both declared illegal, along with the Irish Volunteers, Gaelic League and Cumann na mBan, as well as their journals and newspapers. From then on, the Dáil would hold only a few secret sessions, while the cabinet met 'on the run'. Constance was released on Saturday, 18 October and attended a reception and concert organised by the Irish Women's Franchise League in Dublin to celebrate her release. She was delighted to be back among her friends, returning to live with Kathleen Clarke.

At midnight that day, Constable Michael Downing of the Dublin Metropolitan Police (DMP) was shot dead in High Street, Dublin, after he approached three suspects while on patrol. For some time, 'The Squad', a group of trained assassins recruited by Michael Collins, had targeted members of the DMP's G Division, but Downing was not a member of that division. Tensions in the city rose and Cumann na mBan's annual conference, scheduled for the Mansion House on 20 October, was banned, with twenty DMP constables along with a superintendent, an inspector and two sergeants assigned to patrol Dawson Street. Most republicans stayed away, although Maud Gonne MacBride appeared, as did Countess Plunkett on a tricycle. According to the police reports, Constance stepped off a tram at about 2pm, accompanied by a 'low sized dark sallow-complexioned lady wearing glasses'. She walked up to the Mansion House and, when stopped by a policeman, asked to see the Lord Mayor stating that she was the 'Minister for Labour' under the 'Irish Government' elected by the Irish people.

When asked whether she was connected with the banned meeting, she retorted:

> What meeting? What an impertinent question. Do you represent the hirelings of the British government? What Irishmen! I got four months in Cork for telling people about you and I'm glad I did so! You won't let me in then; very well. I have been here to test it and I hope you won't be too badly punished.

She then walked away towards the Green. The police authorities were not prepared to dismiss Constance's words as the bravado of a woman only just released from prison, describing her as a 'pestilential harridan' from the 'most extreme section' of the republican movement. They believed that her release from Cork jail had been celebrated by the murder of Constable Downing and that she posed a grave danger to public order: 'While she and those associated with her move freely about, assassinations will continue.'

The Dáil met once more on 27 October, with its departments doing their best to continue functioning, despite being banned and under constant surveillance. Constance's Department of Labour was located in North Frederick Street and masqueraded as a letting agency for apartments. It also contained pianos on one floor so women on the staff could pretend to be music teachers if raided. Because of Constance's scrupulous attention to detail, her Ministry was the only Dáil department to escape a raid.

She maintained her connection with the Irish Citizen Army, doing what she could to improve the education of the workers. During that year, she stayed for a time in the house of Thomas Johnson, the first leader of the Labour Party in Dáil Éireann. Some labour activists believed that communism, as preached by Karl Marx, would see a return to a more communal way of life. Among them was Constance, although she had little time for labels. 'We're fighting for the working class,' she would say, 'call us what you like.' Like many traditional Sinn Féiners, she wanted to see a co-operative economy based on agriculture that would reduce the need for imports and see off the 'gombeen' middlemen.

In November 1919, Dublin Castle made an unsuccessful attempt to deport Constance as an alien, seeing her as a continuing danger to the public peace. The Home Secretary had pointed out that it was contrary to established practise to deport a British-born woman. Even worse, it 'might give the lady and her sympathisers a most undesirable advertisement' and it presented considerable practical difficulties. The whereabouts of her husband was unknown; he was either Polish or Russian, but no one knew which and then there was the problem of which country would be willing to take her; France and Holland were among the countries mentioned. Far better to keep control of her under Article 11 of the Aliens Restriction (Amendment) Act 1919, he suggested.

A crackdown in December saw a raid on the house where Constance was living. Dáil Éireann headquarters was raided and the Mansion House, official residence of the lord mayor, was occupied by troops. A total of 187 raids resulted in thirty-two arrests on political charges and nine deportations, although no charges were brought. The annual *Aonach* Christmas Fair was cancelled. No one knew when they would be arrested or for what reason. Constance was away when they came to arrest her. She asked Eva to try and find out what they wanted to charge her with this time – their English cousin, the Communist MP

Cecil L'Estrange Malone might know. She believed that the British were trying to provoke another rebellion so that they could eliminate the problem of Irish nationalism once and for all.

She continued to give the military the slip: 'It's awfully funny being on the run. I don't know whether I am most like the timid hare, the wily fox or a fierce wild animal of the jungle.' She moved from house to house with little difficulty. 'I fly around the town on my bike for exercise and it's too funny seeing the expression on the policemen's faces when they see me whizz by.'

At the end of 1919 came an appeal by Irish women activists to their 'sisters in other countries' for Irish internees to be recognised internationally as political prisoners. The document was signed by Constance for Cumann na mBan, Hanna Sheehy Skeffington for the Irish Women's Franchise League, Helena Molony for the Irish Women Workers' Union, Louie Bennett of the Irishwomen's International League, Maud Gonne MacBride for Inghinidhe na hÉireann, and Kathleen Lynn for the League of Women Delegates. An American Committee for the Relief of Ireland was established and shiploads of food and clothing were sent across the Atlantic, while fundraising continued. By the end of 1922, over £1.5m had been collected. Tensions remained high and, on 19 December, Lord French, the viceroy, was ambushed by Volunteers at Ashtown, just outside the Phoenix Park. One of the Volunteers, Martin Savage, aged twenty-one, was shot dead.

Dáil Éireann continued its effort to run the country while Ireland descended into a state of anarchy. Democratically elected members of the new parliament, most of them civilians, moved from house to house attempting to evade arrest and raids. On the streets, British soldiers, many of them shell-shocked or, at the very least, traumatised after long years in the trenches of Europe, behaved with savage brutality.

Yeats, in his poem 'Nineteen Hundred and Nineteen', put it graphically:

> ... a drunken soldiery
> Can leave the mother, murdered at her door,
> To crawl in her own blood, and go scot-free...

CHAPTER FIFTEEN

The Shadow of a Gunman

Late in 1919, Sinn Féin had begun planning for the municipal elections scheduled for 15 January 1920. For the first time in Ireland, proportional representation would be used in an attempt by the authorities to undercut the republicans. Sinn Féin had no fear of the new system – at the Sinn Féin *ard fheis* held in April, Arthur Griffith, Eoin MacNeill, de Valera and Constance had all spoken in favour of it.

Although Constance attempted to get women to stand, she found them reluctant, many fearing for their own safety and with good reason. Whenever Constance spoke, the army or the police appeared soon after, although she usually managed to evade them. A directive of 14 January 1920 from W. E. Johnstone, Dublin Metropolitan Police Chief Commissioner, reported that Countess Markievicz had made appearances at two unannounced meetings in Dublin over the previous few days. He impressed 'on all who superintend' the grave importance of securing her arrest over the next day or two. 'To this end, enough force must be kept in reserve at Divisional Headquarters and a message sent to G Division the moment an unannounced meeting is discovered'. A motor van would also be kept available. Advice was also given that 'The police on the spot must act firmly and promptly, as the Countess never remains at a meeting for more than a few minutes and may possibly be heavily veiled and, therefore, difficult to recognise. Superintendents are advised to have at least three cyclists trawling the city on the look-out for impromptu meetings.'

In January 1920, under the initials C.M., Constance wrote an article for the *Irish Citizen*, pointing out the right of every family to have a good home, and urging women to vote in the municipal elections. She wanted new houses for workers built at once and her concern mirrored that of Labour and Sinn Féin. Constance advised women to demand a home with a good living room, two or three bedrooms, a boiler, gas cooker and coal cellar. This must have seemed quite luxurious to the working-class women of the time. She believed that living outside the city centre was better for children: 'crime and cruelty is found far less in these beautiful suburbs, where every housewife wears a dignified air of being mistress to a really good home with a lovely garden, where she can grow fruit, vegetables and flowers'. Like fellow nationalists, she saw the future Ireland as a bucolic idyll: 'We do not want a black country with all its slums, misery and crime to be built among the fair hills of Ireland.' Hostility to city life was not unique to Ireland; English and German intellectuals held similar views.

Women, as household managers, should ensure that the house was kept clean and tidy 'no matter however simple and poor it might be'. Constance argued that the state was but a larger version of the home, and advised women of every class to 'arouse themselves and take the keenest interest to abolish all slums and to see in Dublin a city built worthy of the lovely mountains and the surrounding country and sea'.

In another article, Constance appealed to women to start campaigning against assaults on children. Judging such cases, especially when they concerned girls, was proving problematic because most of the officers of the law, although they meant well, were men, as Constance had seen for herself when attending court cases. Women magistrates and solicitors were needed to counteract this bias. She liked to give women jobs and felt her time in jail had helped bring women into the open: 'The shyest are ready to do my work when I'm not there.'

A child, representing the future, was the responsibility not just of the parents but also of the community. She pointed out that it was mostly working women who were driven to desperate acts when their children were cold and hungry and who then ended up in jail, as she had witnessed at Aylesbury. Education was the key: 'only when all children of a nation have the same education will they have the same chances in life and learn to look after the people as a whole'. Working-class mothers were in a desperate situation, especially when their men were on the run. She commented that 'the whole economic position of

Ireland has reduced our workers to such a terrible state of poverty and uncertainty that one bows in admiration to the splendid mothers of the lovely children that they have given to Ireland with such unthinkable suffering and self-denial'.

Although she helped out at St Ultan's, the children's hospital Kathleen Lynn had founded at Charlemont Street in 1919, Constance had little to say about maternity and birth control clinics, possibly reflecting the predominantly Catholic ethos of the Dáil and the puritanism of the time. Nor did Constance demand state welfare, although she had supported the abolition of Poor Law doles and the provision of a widow's pension in her election campaign.

A total of forty-three women were elected to local councils and boroughs. Of the thirty-three county councils, twenty-nine had Sinn Féin majorities, along with 172 rural district councils, all of them pledging allegiance to Dáil Éireann. Republican justices or 'Brehons' were often women, among them Hanna Sheehy Skeffington, president of the Court of Conscience at Dublin Corporation. Anne Ceannt and Áine Heron served in Rathmines Pembroke before it was amalgamated with Dublin Corporation, and Kathleen Clarke was elected alderman for both the Wood Quay and Mountjoy wards. Yet there was a feeling that women's involvement in public affairs was merely a product of the extraordinary times. The important administrative, political and military decisions were still taken by men.

Overall, eleven of the twelve Irish cities voted republican in the election; Belfast was the only exception. The British continued to ignore the clear wishes of the people, as they had done after the general election. Every day came new tales of raids and reprisals. The military and the police continued to harass republicans, roaming the street with what Constance called 'covered wagons', rounding up and searching suspected republicans and, with bayonets fixed, charging at curious civilians who may have gathered, knocking women and children to the ground and causing untold injuries.

With the *Irish Bulletin*, the Dáil's official gazette, publicising details of British acts of aggression, international concern was increasing. Several fact-finding missions came to Ireland, registering a damning catalogue of brutality, destruction and murder in an atmosphere of sheer terror. After its visit in November 1920, the British Labour Party called for the withdrawal of British troops and the setting up of an Irish Constituent Assembly. Its appeal was ignored.

Constance was now fifty-two years of age and occasionally her cheerful mask slipped:

> It is rather wearying when the English Man Pack are in full cry after you, though I get a lot of fun out of it ... I have had some very narrow shaves. The other night, I knocked around with a raiding party and watched them insult the crowd. I was among the people and I went right up to Store Street Police Barracks where the military and the police lined up before going home. Night after night they wake people up and carry off someone, they don't seem to mind who. Some of the people they took lately did not belong to our crowd at all.

She became adept at disguise – a favourite was a particular Victorian bonnet that transformed her into a fragile old woman. She was recognised but never betrayed even when, on one memorable occasion, she raced for a tram, lifting up her long skirt. Nora Connolly remembered a trip with 'granny' into Dublin's city centre. Constance, with a gleam of mischief in her eye, hopped nervously on and off the footpath until an unwary policeman escorted her across Sackville Street.

There was a much-told tale of her hiding incriminating documents in plain view. Hearing a raid was imminent, Constance stuffed her papers into a trunk, hailed a taxi and, after some thought, brought it to a friend who owned a pawn shop. There the trunk was placed in the front window with an elevated price tag so that no one would be tempted to buy it.

In March 1920, Constance went to stay with the O'Carroll family. 'Auntie' remained for eight months and was remembered by the family for her enthusiastic gardening and her attempts to learn the Irish language. She soon threw off her little old lady disguise and returned to the work of her department, Mrs O'Carroll reported.

On 1 March, in a letter asking for support for the Republican Loan, she described the difficulties Ireland's representatives were having, with collectors in constant danger of imprisonment: 'On mutual trust and mutual help our Republic is being built up – a trust founded on our mutual love of Ireland and sanctified by our mutual participation in the Great Awakening when the Republic was proclaimed from the GPO in Easter Week 1916.'

Despite the best efforts of the British, Sinn Féin was quietly establishing itself as the government of the country. The Republican courts, functioning all over the country, had earned a reputation for fairness and became widely popular; cases appearing before the Assizes shrivelled. Running the courts was not easy since, wherever they were held, raids by the British military could be expected. The Republican Loan was heavily subscribed, despite its underground nature. Although they subpoenaed nearly every bank manager in Dublin, the British could not discover where the fund was kept and, when they brought in a detective, Alan Bell, to investigate, he was shot dead within a month by one of Collins's men.

Lessons had been learned from 1916 and the war against the British occupier was led not by armies but by 'Flying Columns' – small groups of guerrilla fighters who could move quickly, attack and then disappear. For a young man with an adventurous streak, membership of a 'Flying Column' was exhilarating; they lived as outlaws, sleeping in barns and fields and cadging food from sympathisers. Overseeing the new militancy was Michael Collins, who had stepped into the leadership vacuum when de Valera left for the USA in June 1919. In Dublin, Collins continued to operate his own 'executions squad'; his men posed as builders' labourers, wearing guns under aprons. Like Constance, Collins was miraculously invisible. He had spies everywhere.

As usual in war, it was the civilians who suffered: 'Shot in the back to save the British Empire, an' shot in the breast to save the soul of Ireland,' the character Seumas Shields says in Seán O'Casey's play, *The Shadow of a Gunman*. Shields expressed the views of many neutrals: 'I'm a Nationalist meself right enough ... but I draw the line when I hear the gunmen blowin' about dyin' for the people, when it's the people that are dyin' for the gunmen!' Many rebels and their families took to sleeping in the fields by night. Women were dragged into a conflict over which they had no control. All they could do was wait for news of their husbands, fathers, sons and brothers; it left many feeling helpless and bitter.

By February 1920, there had been 5,000 raids, over 500 arrests and ninety-eight towns sacked and burned. A total of 203 were killed by the British forces and 48,474 families had their homes raided. Of the seventy-two Sinn Féin members of parliament, sixty-four had been arrested and a further two deported. The six remaining, including de Valera, were abroad. A curfew from midnight to 5am was extended to 8pm to 5am. In April 1920, prisoners in Mountjoy went on hunger strike and, after eleven days, they were released, helped by a general strike in Dublin. The British were starting to show some respect for Sinn Féin.

During the last days of March 1920, the English cabinet had adopted a more aggressively military policy in Ireland, with Sir Nevil Macready appointed as Commander-in-Chief of the English Army of Occupation in Ireland. Because they were opposed to this policy, three Royal Irish Constabulary (RIC) officials were asked to retire. In the five months following, 133 Irish towns and villages were sacked, shot up or partially burned. Policing became a problem because of the dwindling number of local people signing up for the RIC, with barracks in many rural areas closing. To boost their number, the British had opened the ranks to the thousands of ex-soldiers who had failed to find work after the war, often with good reason. Because the dark green uniform of the RIC was in short supply, these new recruits were given Army khaki with an RIC cap and belt. They became known as the 'Black and Tans'. RIC officers had little notion of how to deal with the unruly ex-soldiers, many of them working-class Londoners, who had no experience of community policing, let alone rural life.

The Black and Tans were followed by an even more fearsome force: the Auxiliaries. These former army officers, wearing blue uniforms and glengarry caps, were paid £1 a day, compared to the ten shillings given to the Black and Tans. While the Republicans hated the Black and Tans, they both loathed and feared the Auxiliaries who were often drunk and, on the flimsiest of excuses, repeatedly assaulted men and women alike in a vicious manner. Although the Lord Lieutenant estimated that there were at least 100,000 Sinn Féin members, only 15,000 of these – at most – were in 'active service'. They would have to employ all their ingenuity to deal with a well-organised British army of 20,000, and a further force of 20,000 policemen.

One effective method of hampering British army movements was employed by Transport Union staff who, in the six months from May 1920, refused to work on trains carrying the British army or to handle military equipment or stores at the docks. Sinn Féin also benefited from a superb intelligence system, including spies in Dublin Castle, organised by Michael Collins.

In May 1920, Dublin Corporation, dominated by Republicans, acknowledged the authority of the Dáil as the duly elected government of Ireland. That month, Constance received a death threat 'from the Black Hand gang in the police'. It was printed on paper 'they had taken the precaution of stealing from us'. She wrote to a friend that the police were clearly plotting to murder her and others, and were manufacturing evidence 'to prove that we assassinated each other'. In the same letter, she reports that, at the annual Fianna *Aeraiocht*: 'The boys made Aunt Sallies in the form of hideous caricatures of police and soldiers painted on boards – these were a great attraction'. On 14 May, she defied the authorities when she made a dramatic appearance at an open-air meeting in Croke Park held to commemorate the dead leaders of 1916. In June, she attended the annual Wolfe Tone commemoration at Bodenstown.

On 29 June 1920, the Dáil met for the first time since October; it was maintaining its efforts to function as the respectable face of nationalism, with TDs wearing suits and carrying briefcases. With de Valera still in the USA, Arthur Griffith presided. He highlighted the success of the National Land Bank, which had helped settle a land crisis in the west of Ireland, as well as of the Land Arbitration Courts and the Industrial Commission. As Minister for Finance, Michael Collins had managed the greatest feat of all – the Republican Loan was over-subscribed by £40,000.

Earlier that month, on 19 June, Colonel Gerald Smyth, recently appointed divisional commissioner of police for Munster, had made an explosive speech at the RIC barracks in Listowel – the only police barracks in Munster that had refused to co-operate with the military. Forgetting that he was addressing policemen, not soldiers, he advised officers to do their best to wipe out Sinn Féin. If a police barracks was burned down, then the RIC was to take over the biggest house in the locality and throw the occupants in the gutter. If civilians on the roads did not respond to a 'Hands Up' order, they were to be shot: 'innocent persons may be shot, but that cannot be helped ... The more you shoot the better I will like you.' His listeners were aghast and when Constable Jeremiah Mee was asked whether he was prepared to co-operate, he removed his cap, belt and bayonet and called Smyth a murderer. Smyth ordered his arrest, but backed off when Mee's comrades swore the room would run with blood if the order was carried out. Mee and thirteen others immediately resigned. Other Munster barracks stood by their Listowel comrades.

Not until 10 July was Smyth's speech printed in the *Freeman's Journal*, with explosive effect. A day later, Mee and some of his colleagues went to Dublin to meet Dáil members, among them Michael Collins and Constance, in the offices of the Irish Labour Party. In Westminster, Lloyd George, after promising a full investigation into the incident, called Colonel Smyth back to London. Two days after his visit, Colonel Smyth was shot dead by the Irish Republican Army (IRA) at Cork County Club. His funeral in Banbridge, County Down on 20 July was followed by a three-day pogrom against local Catholic homes and businesses, with one Protestant man shot dead and three Irish nationalists convicted of firearms offences.

Patience was running short on all sides. The daily newspapers of 24 July announced that, in future, hunger strikers would not be released until they had served their full term of imprisonment and that the holding of inquests on Sinn Féin victims would be made illegal. Colonel Smyth may have been dead but the policy he had outlined in Listowel was very much alive.

Between July and September 1920, the Labour ministry sorted out 129 strikes. Constance came to believe that workers all too often opted to go on strike without any coherent policy, distracting attention from the fight for Irish independence, which she still saw as fundamental. She supported strikes that could weaken British control, such as the munitions transport strike. Workers' living conditions needed attention and the ministry decided to investigate the wages and hours of employees in agriculture, industry and commerce. Unemployment was a critical problem, with another recession biting and 100,000 jobless. Among them were hundreds of ex-RIC men; about 1,590 RIC men resigned in 1920 alone.

Unrest in the countryside remained a concern and she proposed investigating farm profits, establishing co-ops and taking over the Irish Packing Company; all practical ideas. The cabinet listened and did nothing. Constance ran into trouble with a fishing co-op in Kerry, where money went astray. Even with co-ops, difficulties could arise: 'The old problem always remains: how to prevent all the money and power, etc. getting into the hands of a few, and they establishing themselves as a ruling tyrant class.'

During the land agitation of 1920, Constance helped to settle a number of land disputes. She seconded a proposal to distribute vacant land and farms to the unemployed and landless. This was not supported, largely because Sinn Féin had its heartland in rural areas, where the 'big farmers' created most of the country's wealth. In the Dáil sessions of 6 August and 17 September, ministers heard of more arrests and reprisals, and also of attacks on creameries, mills and bacon factories as part of British strategy to slow the economy.

Lissadell had experienced its own labour problems, with Alderman John Jinks of Sligo recruiting farm workers for the Irish Transport and General Workers' Union and calling for a strike after a dispute about conditions. Constance wrote to Josslyn, reminding him that he came from a family of 'tyrants and usurpers'. Josslyn was far more concerned about the plight of his dairy cows, which had to be milked twice a day. When the workmen came back to work, they milked the cows on to the ground. There were also IRA raids; in one, which took place while the family was at church, the raiders failed to find the guns they were looking for, but took Josslyn's favourite gun case, which he later found hidden in a gorse bush.

Over the summer, Constance broke the curfew to visit Alfie Byrne, who spent much of his time travelling between Ireland and England attempting to help political prisoners. After tapping on his window, she handed him a roll of music that contained a warning for nine of 'our boys' in London who were going to be arrested. Byrne immediately set out for London and reached the men before the police.

Early in August, Constance summonsed Jeremiah Mee to her office at 14 North Frederick Street, receiving him with Michael Collins 'in the most friendly manner'. She wanted him to take charge of a bureau she was setting up to find jobs for ex-RIC members. Mee was given his own room and Constance delighted in introducing him as 'an RIC man from Kerry' to the prominent IRA men who came to meet her. Although initially Collins was not ready to trust Mee, after a month, he admitted that his first impressions were wrong.

Mee found Constance 'a grand person to work with' and one of the few to understand that 'the question of the RIC was an economic rather than a political one'. With Mee's help, she composed a letter to likely employers seeking work for ex-RIC men 'as clerks, agricultural workers, stewards, watchmen, agents, motor drivers, caretakers, etc'. She placed advertisements in the daily papers, with the authorities interpreting this as 'spreading disaffection among His Majesty's Forces', an offence punishable under the Defence of the Realm Act. To boost morale within the police force, the British authorities, led by Chief Secretary Hamar Goodwood, started a paper called Sir Hamar Greenwood's *Weekly Summary*, in which both Constance and Mee figured prominently.

On 26 September 1920, Constance went on a brief trip to Wicklow with Seán MacBride, who was bringing a French writer, Maurice Bourgeois, to see his mother Maud Gonne. When she heard of the trip, Constance insisted on joining them. MacBride was driving a borrowed car that kept breaking down and on their return to Dublin, the car was stopped in Rathmines by police because of a faulty tail lamp. When MacBride admitted he did not have a permit to drive the car, the police lit a match and, peering into the car, realised that one of the passengers was the notorious Madame Markievicz. Also in the car, along with Bourgeois, was a stranger who had missed the last tram and was walking home when offered a lift. 'All the King's horses and all the King's men with great pomp and many large guns' then arrived and a weary night in prison followed for all four. Bourgeois was in Ireland to collect material for the French War Museum and to write articles on Ireland. When he arrived, he had been hostile to Sinn Féin, but after spending two days in a filthy cell, despite showing his diplomatic passport, he became one of the organisation's stoutest champions.

Constance found herself back in Mountjoy Gaol, where she was to spend ten trying weeks with no access to painting materials and limited visitors. Her first thoughts were of her sister, then in Italy, and she wrote to Jennie Wyse Power asking her to send Eva a postcard assuring her that she was well. She added that she was attempting to learn Irish but found it difficult. Her Department of Labour continued its work firstly with Joe McGrath and, after he in turn was arrested, with Joe McDonagh.

While she was in jail, the focus of the world again turned on Ireland with the death on 25 October of Terence MacSwiney, the Lord Mayor of Cork, on the seventy-fourth day of a marathon hunger strike. MacSwiney had been arrested, along with ten others, on 12 August at a meeting in Cork and he had been charged with possessing documents that might 'cause disaffection to His Majesty'. With the others, he went on hunger strike in protest at the continuing arrest of public representatives. On the third day, MacSwiney was taken to Brixton Jail. On 17 October, Michael Fitzgerald, one of the hunger strikers, died. MacSwiney lived for eight more days; within a few hours, Michael Murphy, aged only twenty-two, also died.

Thousands turned out when MacSwiney's tricolour-draped coffin was paraded through the streets of London accompanied by an honour guard of Irish Volunteers. On 31 October, he was buried in Cork. Constance wrote to Joseph McGarrity, a leading member of the Clan na Gael organisation in the United States, about MacSwiney's death: '[t]here is exaltation and joy in the fighter's death, with the passion and glory of the battlefield, but to lie in a prison cell ... requires a courage and strength that is God-like'.

The day after, on 1 November, Kevin Barry, an eighteen-year-old medical student, was hanged in Mountjoy Gaol; he was the first republican to be convicted under the new Restoration of Order to Ireland Act, by which republicans would be tried by military court martial. Barry had been part of a group that had ambushed a party of armed British soldiers during which one of the soldiers had been shot dead. Although there was evidence that Barry's gun had jammed and that he could not have been the killer, he was tortured before his execution by a hangman brought over from England. No local would touch Barry. In a poem she wrote at the time, Constance describes Barry as 'simple and pure and brave'.

Three weeks later, in the early hours of Sunday, 21 November, fourteen British MI5 officers, linked to the Cairo Gang of undercover agents, were shot dead on Collins's orders at various locations in Dublin, many of them in their beds. A further six were injured. Retaliation was swift. Croke Park was the location that afternoon of a big football match and the stands were full. With the match already underway, the

Black and Tans appeared and began shooting into the crowd. Hundreds were injured in the panic and, when the firing stopped, twelve lay dead, with another sixty wounded. It was a miracle that more had not died. From her prison cell in Mountjoy, Constance could hear the sound of the machine guns, reminding her of Easter Week. That night, three IRA men were shot 'while trying to escape' from the guard room at Dublin Castle. At the inquest it was clear that they had been beaten to death. An editorial in the *New Statesman* of 30 November wholeheartedly condemned the murder, theft and arson committed by the Black and Tans and the 'state of government terrorism' prevailing in Ireland.

In the autumn of 1920, the Manchester branch of the Women's International League had organised a fact-finding mission to Ireland. Following the publication of its report, a series of public meetings were held in England with 'magic lantern' slides of ruined homes and burned out-shops and buildings illustrating the shocking conditions. Resolutions were sent to the government demanding the liberation of prisoners and a truce.

On 2 December, Constance's courtmartial in front of eight judges began at the Royal Barracks. Based on Fianna literature found in a raid the previous September at 26 Nassau Street, where Eamon Martin was living, she was charged with organising the Fianna ten years earlier. In the courtroom were Maud Gonne MacBride, Hanna Sheehy Skeffington, Kathleen Lynn and the war correspondent Henry Nevinson. Photographers who took pictures were asked to surrender the plates.

On the second day in court, Constance cross-examined witnesses. She asked for proof that any Fianna boy had ever attacked the British armed forces. She denied the allegation that she was responsible for the shooting of a policeman who had arrested her. Since Easter week, she said, terrible things had been put into her mouth that she had never had a chance to disprove: 'I am willing to sacrifice everything to Ireland except my good name.'

She was sentenced to two years' hard labour on Christmas Eve and wrote to Eva telling her not to bother about her:

> As you know, the English ideal of modern civilisation always galled me. Endless relays of exquisite food and the eternal changing of costume bored me always to tears and I prefer my own to so many

people's company ... I have my health and I can always find a way to give my dreams a living form. So I sit and dream and build up a world of birds and butterflies and flowers from a sheen in a dew drop or the flash of a seagull's wing.

During the previous year, ninety-eight civilians had been killed by unprovoked fire, thirty-six assassinated while in prison and sixty-nine shot in their beds or on the street. The British public was beginning to express its revulsion. Still the violence continued. In December 1920, martial law was proclaimed in Cork, Kerry, Tipperary and Limerick and later extended to all the Munster counties as well as to Kilkenny and Wexford. Soldiers arrested and destroyed almost at random; anyone caught with guns or ammunition was liable to be executed. On the night of 11 December, Auxiliaries set fire to Cork city centre, and the city hall and downtown shopping area were destroyed. In the censored press, the fire was attributed to natural causes. Explosions, gunfire and violence had become a way of life in Ireland.

On 23 December 1920, the Government of Ireland Act became law. It allowed for two parliaments: one in Dublin, one in Belfast. During the year, British politicians had considered a bill that would provide for two parliaments linked by a joint council, with some powers reserved for the British parliament. That month, de Valera finally returned to Ireland after eighteen months in the USA. During his absence, the political landscape in Ireland had altered. Hardline republicans, including Constance, opposed the Government of Ireland Act. She pointed out that the ultimate powers under the bill were 'vested in a viceroy and a Privy council who are merely servants of the British Cabinet'. Ireland would have no control of its finances or of its industries. A total of £18m in Irish taxes would go to London 'for England's debts'. The British army of occupation would 'continue to terrorise, murder, insult and rob our people'. In summary, the proposed Irish parliament would be little more than a talking shop.

After she had been in jail for two months, Constance was joined by Eithne Coyle, a Gaelic League organiser originally from Donegal, but working in Longford and later in Roscommon. Coyle was arrested on New Year's Eve 1920 and, on 29 February 1921, was sentenced to three years' penal servitude for aiding IRA members. Coyle remembered

Constance's love of gardening and how she had asked for dung. Several sacks of manure were delivered, helping her to grow both sweet peas and eating peas, despite the starlings and pigeons 'making war on everything'. She was continuing her study of the Irish language and was on the fifth book of 'O'Growney' when Coyle arrived. Already in Mountjoy was Eileen McGrane, a lecturer at University College Dublin, who had also been arrested on New Year's Eve, along with Máire Rigney and Lily Dunne. Later, the Sharkey sisters and Peg McGuinness arrived from Athlone Barracks, followed by Linda Kearns from prison in England, along with Frances Brady and Molly Hyland.

The horrors continued. On 14 March, six men were executed in Mountjoy after an attack on an RIC patrol in Drumcondra, Dublin. In April, Father Sweetman visited Constance in Mountjoy, bringing a gift from Eva of a green and silver rosary blessed by Pope Benedict XV in Rome. Because of Eva's deteriorating health, she and Esther Roper had spent much of the previous year in Italy and, while in Rome, they had stayed with the Irish Papal Envoy, George Gavan Duffy, and his wife, Margaret.

On 24 May 1921, elections under the Government of Ireland Act were held. Sinn Féin took part in the elections but refused to recognise the two parliaments. Instead the party treated the elections in both parts of Ireland as elections to the Second Dáil, which would govern one united country. Since none of the 128 candidates put forward in the south were opposed, no polling took place. The 124 Sinn Féin candidates and the four from Trinity College would make up the Second Dáil; Constance was joined by five other women – Mary MacSwiney, Ada English, Kathleen Clarke, Kate O'Callaghan and Margaret Pearse.

Constance watched and listened from her prison cell. She never gave up hope:

> Italy certainly fills one with hope, Greece too and Poland. We are the only ones left in chains ... it all makes one feel that we must win; the spiritual must prevail over the material in the end; we suffer, and suffering unites us and teaches us to stand by each other. It also makes us friends everywhere, while the policies of our enemies is leaving them friendless.

On 15 May 1921, Lord French was replaced as viceroy by Lord FitzAlan, the first Catholic to hold the position. In June 1921, the Government of Northern Ireland was formally established and, on 24 June, Prime Minister Lloyd George wrote to Éamon de Valera proposing peace discussions. A truce came into force on 11 July. Three days later, de Valera met Lloyd George in London. Constance knew little of what was happening and, in one of her final prison letters, she wrote of her plans for her rock garden.

On Sunday, 24 July, with the Truce now in operation, Constance was told by the Mountjoy prison governor that she was free to go. Eithne Coyle had become so devoted to her that she cried for a week after she left and was comforted with drinks of hot milk by a friendly wardress. Constance was now homeless. St Mary's had been rented out for many years, but Josslyn had been forced to sell the house to help pay for his rebel sister's expenses. She had nothing left of material value.

CHAPTER SIXTEEN

'I have seen the stars'

Constance revelled in her freedom: 'It is almost worthwhile being locked up, for the great joy release brings.'

With the British army back in their barracks and freedom fighters no longer on the run, she returned to work at the Department of Labour. From February 1921, the Department had organised an economic boycott of Belfast after thousands of Catholics working in the Belfast shipyards were forced from their jobs. Tensions had been high since July 1920 when, after the killing of a northern police officer in Cork, loyalists (many of them unemployed ex-servicemen) marched on the city's shipyards to force up to 7,000 Catholic workers and their 'rotten Prod' sympathisers from their jobs. From mid-1920 to the autumn of 1922, 465 people died and over a thousand were wounded in sectarian outrages and riots.

Constance opposed the boycott; she believed that splitting Ireland into two trading centres would play into British hands, giving them a good excuse for partition. Nor would it help trade union attempts to unite workers from all religious backgrounds against their common enemy. Despite warnings, not just from Constance but from Ernest Blythe and Arthur Griffith, a groundswell of local support ensured that boycotts began in various locations around the country. In March 1921, there were 184 boycott committees; by May that number had climbed to 360.

When it came to labour relations, the Department of Labour continued to work closely with the unions in attempting to resolve disputes through a series of conciliation boards. Among the arbitrators were Darrell Figgis, Tom Kelly, Ernest Blythe and Seán Moylan. Disputes ranged from the agricultural – the harvest bonus for farm workers – to disagreements in factories, offices and shops. Constance was deeply troubled by instances of religious bigotry, as in one case when the Catholic owner of a quarry in the north ordered his manager to dismiss a Protestant worker. She threatened to put such matters in the hands of the police if they were not resolved.

Despite the prevailing air of optimism, neither side was convinced that the truce would hold. Many republicans were still in jail and, of the 3,200 who were interned, including forty women, fewer than half had been tried. Among the women, mostly imprisoned for possessing Cumann na mBan literature, were two sisters called Cotter and their cousin, who were weeding turnips in a field when a Black and Tan lorry was blown up nearby. Elderly sisters, one aged seventy and the other eighty, from Ballinalee were briefly held for harbouring Seán McKeon after an ambush. Mary Bowles, aged fourteen, from County Cork, got five years for 'endeavouring to save a machine gun from capture'.

The Bolshevik revolution in Russia was attracting wide coverage at the time and affecting political thought. Britain, enjoying a post-war boom, and with its political system relatively unscathed, despite the war, was hit by a series of strikes that were giving hope to socialist revolutionaries such as Sylvia Pankhurst, whose *Dreadnought* magazine Constance read while in prison. In October 1921, Constance sent a memorandum to the cabinet warning of the imminence of social revolution. She feared a sequence of events, starting with 'small outbreaks growing more and more frequent and violent, the immediate result of which will tend to disrupt the Republican cause'. All that was needed was a 'violent popular leader'. She had been reading Lenin, who believed that a revolution could only be achieved by the strong leadership of one person, or of a very select few, over the masses.

Her busy life of speeches and meetings meant that the only time she had to read and ponder was when she was in prison. She reflected that Ireland had 'never produced a tyrant'. There was, in the Irish nature, a feeling for 'decentralisation' that she equated with modern 'soviets' or worker-led social groupings. That streak had also prevented the Irish from ever getting together 'under one head'.

After de Valera's negotiations with Ulster and London, interned members of the Dáil were released on 6 August so they could meet and discuss the terms of Lloyd George's proposals for the truce. Constance, influenced by meeting the mother of a boy killed in the fighting, did not condemn the proposals outright.

Although she had retained her seat in the elections, Constance lost her cabinet position when de Valera, appointed as president, reduced the cabinet to seven – Michael Collins, Arthur Griffith, Austin Stack, Cathal Brugha, William Cosgrave and Robert Barton. A further nine ministers were appointed, with Constance remaining Secretary for Labour. When de Valera proposed a constitutional amendment to ratify the cabinet changes, Kate O'Callaghan vigorously opposed the demotion of the only female member of the cabinet. She was supported by Mary MacSwiney, who warned that it would set a dangerous precedent. She was right – not until 1979 would another Irish woman, Máire Geoghegan-Quinn, be given full ministerial office.

The October 1921 convention of Cumann na mBan – the first since 1917 that was not suppressed – was its largest ever. With memories of the War of Independence still raw, the convention took place in an atmosphere of battle-weary determination. Constance, presiding for the first time in four years, argued that it was time for action not speeches; women must be ready to fight. She believed that the struggle was far from over and women were instructed to

> go out and work as if war was going to break out next week ... go and prepare yourselves to do good work for Ireland in the way you have done it in the past. Put yourselves in touch with your local Volunteers, avoid quarrelling, look over deficiencies, and try and work everywhere together wherever you can.

Cumann na mBan had evolved. Women, active participants in the war, felt that they had earned the right to be consulted about the peace. Members were more politically aware and capable of holding their own in debates, while restructuring meant that each Irish Republican Army company had a Cumann na mBan branch attached to it. Some tensions remained. Women were not screened as thoroughly as men and had a separate oath: 'I pledge myself to support and defend to the best of my ability the Irish Republic and to uphold the aims and objects of Cumann na mBan and the IRA'. Yet, since members tended to come from staunchly republican families well known in their localities, problems with informers did not arise. Few women had the freedom to uproot themselves and start afresh elsewhere, as men did.

On Hallowe'en 1921, Eithne Coyle, along with Linda Kearns, Eileen Keogh and May Burke, slung a rope ladder over the Mountjoy Gaol wall and escaped, with other women playing a football match to distract the warders. Waiting were the cars of St John Gogarty and Dr Pat McLaverty. One of the helpers was a petty criminal called Seamus Burke, whom Michael Collins rightly suspected of being a British spy. After lying low in the McLaverty house for a week, Coyle and Keogh arrived at the home of Maud Gonne MacBride in St Stephen's Green. One of their first visitors was Constance, who gave Eithne £5 to tide her over, telling her she need not pay it back. Coyle repaid her at the first opportunity. Next stop was a convent in Kilcullen, County Kildare, but when Burke's double dealings were discovered, the escapees were quickly moved to an IRA camp in Carlow. While there, the pair received a letter from Constance, representing the Cumann na mBan executive. After a complaint from Eileen McGrane, they were to be court-martialled for escaping without informing the other women prisoners, a charge that Coyle strenuously denied. The charge was later dropped.

To her great joy, Constance had, at last, received a letter from her husband, now settled in Warsaw and working as legal advisor and commercial counsellor to the American Consulate General, as well as writing and producing plays. The family home at Zywotowka had been burnt down by the Bolsheviks and the family had scattered. After five years' service with the Imperial Marine Guards, her stepson Staskou had married a Russian woman, Alexandra Ivanova Zimina, in the Orthodox church, but because the Bolsheviks did not recognise the union, Alexandra could not get Polish identity papers. The couple lost a newborn baby to typhus in the hard winter of 1920. In January 1921, Staskou was arrested by the Bolsheviks and held prisoner for twenty-five months. His wife left him to his fate.

Always conscious of the police censor, Constance replied in neutral tones to her husband's letter, giving the Mansion House, Dawson Street, as an address. She made inquiries about Casimir's family, reported on their furniture and hoped that, if the truce held, he might come and visit. In reply to his question about her plans, she wrote that she had none because it was impossible to make any 'at a time like this'. She had come into contact with 'many of the old acting crowd' in recent times and everyone was asking for him. 'I'm so sorry to hear about Stas. I wonder why anybody considers it wrong to marry the girl you love. Surely it was not political, he hated politics so.' She ended by asking him to write again soon, before signing off 'Yours ever'.

Constance had stayed with friends in Percy Place for a few months after the Truce. Early in the winter, she moved in with the Coghlans at Frankfort House in Rathgar – close to where she had lived with Casimir when they had come to Dublin some twenty years earlier. The Coghlan children were told that a Mrs Murray was coming to stay and, for ever after, she was Auntie Murray. In October, she was re-elected president of Cumann na mBan.

Negotiations for the terms of a treaty agreeable to both the British and the Irish were continuing. After a protracted exchange of letters, a conference was arranged. Trade, defence and Ireland's association with the British Commonwealth were key points to be discussed.

On 7 October 1921, the five Irish delegates to the conference were given their credentials. They were Arthur Griffith, Michael Collins, Robert Barton, Edmund Duggan and George Gavan Duffy; Duggan and Duffy were the legal advisors. Appointed as secretaries were Erskine Childers, Finian Lynch, Diarmuid O'Hegarty and John Chartres. Making up the British delegation were Lloyd George, Lord Birkenhead, Sir Laming Worthington-Evans, Austen Chamberlain, Winston Churchill and Sir Hamar Greenwood. De Valera's refusal to join the delegation has been debated ever since. After his talks with Lloyd George, he knew that there was no chance of the British approving an Irish republic. There was a good chance of the talks collapsing; if that happened, he believed that it would force further negotiations and, at that point, he might become involved and introduce his plan to leave Ireland outside the inner circle of the Commonwealth while maintaining contact with it. He believed this 'external association' solution would be an acceptable compromise for both the British negotiators and the republican 'die-hards'.

The Irish delegates were given instructions to 'negotiate and conclude on behalf of Ireland a treaty or treaties of settlement, association and accommodation between Ireland and the British Commonwealth'. While they had full power to negotiate, the draft treaty would be sent to Dublin for review before it was signed.

From 11 October until 6 December – eight weeks in all – the marathon negotiations continued in London. It was to prove an exhausting process with long days of meetings punctuated by frequent trips across the Irish Sea by the delegates; this would not have been necessary had de Valera agreed to travel. Telephone calls were not considered an option because of the risk of tapping. Undertaking most of the hard negotiating were Griffith and Collins. By the end of November, a rough draft of a treaty was hammered out. The new Irish Free State would have far greater powers than before but would give up its aspiration to a 32-county Ireland.

Under the eighteen articles of agreement, the Irish Free State would have its own parliament and executive. It would enjoy the same constitutional status as Canada, Australia, New Zealand and South Africa, with its representatives taking an oath of allegiance to the Crown. The country would have religious and educational freedom. Ireland would have its own army, although strategically important harbours, among them Queenstown (now Cobh), would remain in British hands. Britain would also have access to Irish airports and airspace.

The critical article concerned the status of 'Northern Ireland', which would have the right to decide whether it would remain separate from the Irish Free State. Should the North reject incorporation into the new state, a boundary commission would establish a border. When the Dáil met to discuss the document on 3 December, hard-line republicans refused to acknowledge the many concessions gained by the negotiators, as well as the potential for more in the future. They preferred to dwell on the negatives. They argued that Ireland would not have full fiscal independence, it would have no independent foreign policy and that its defence would lie largely in British hands.

The majority were prepared to live with the proposed terms, which went far further than any Home Rule bill. More difficult to resolve were the questions of an oath of allegiance to the king and the issue of splitting the country in two. De Valera argued that, with this treaty, Griffith had achieved neither full independence nor the national unity for which Republicans had fought so hard. He was less concerned about the oath, which he believed was meaningless. Collins agreed; he described the oath as the sugar coating on the pill. Others, most notably Cathal Brugha, emphatically did not agree. An appeal to de Valera to return with the delegates to London was rejected.

So it was that the weary delegates took the mailboat and train back to London, with no solid idea of the cabinet's position on key issues. After a heated debate on the issue of Ireland remaining in the Empire, which provoked a walk-out by the British negotiators, the Irish argued again for an oath to the Irish Free State rather than to the Crown – a formula suggested by de Valera. Finally, at 2.30am on 6 December, under threat of 'immediate and terrible war' from the Ulster Unionists, the exhausted Irish delegates climbed down and signed the treaty, without referring to the Dáil. Lloyd George, theatrically waving two letters and asking which one he would send to William Craig in the morning, had lived up to his reputation as 'the Welsh wizard'. He had outmanoeuvred the Irish.

Griffith and Collins were realists; they believed that the deal was the best they could negotiate under the circumstances and were aware that a fledging Irish Republic could be crushed in days if the British decided to renew hostilities, although this was unlikely since the British public had no appetite for further conflict, nor could the country afford the expense. The British had played a strategic game; in a volatile and changing world, the Treaty was a warning to other annexed states like India and Egypt that complete independence was not an option. Yet had the negotiators held out against the lurid and unlikely threat of a unionist invasion, some of the finer detail in the Treaty, such as the contentious issue of the Boundary Commission, might have been worked out in a more satisfactory manner.

In Dublin, de Valera was angry that the cabinet had not been consulted one final time. He failed to appreciate that negotiations, especially those held over a long period away from home, take on a life of their own. Both Griffith and Collins were heavy drinkers and all the plenipotentiaries were exhausted after months of shuttling back and forth across the Irish Sea. They wanted an end to it.

Hard-line republicans, including Constance, Cathal Brugha and Austin Stack, felt the Treaty was a betrayal of the Republic that they asserted had been in place since Easter 1916. With the cabinet split, de Valera issued a public letter on 9 December stating that he could not recommend acceptance of the Treaty. The following day, the influential 1st Southern Division of the IRA in Cork, although answerable to the Dáil, made it clear that it would not support the Treaty. Although most Irish people – businessmen, the bigger farmers, the press, the labour movement, army leaders and the Catholic Church – responded favourably to the Treaty, de Valera and the hard-liners continued to argue that it went against the majority opinion as expressed in the recent election.

After the delegates returned to Dublin, ten long and often acrimonious sessions of the Dáil took place in the Council Chamber of University College Dublin at Earlsfort Terrace. Private meetings on 17 and 20 December were followed by the first public sessions running from 19 to 22 December. From the start, a deep chasm appeared between the views of the pragmatists who supported the treaty and the idealists who still clung to the notion of a mythical Irish Republic. As the sessions wore on, speeches became fractious and personal.

Constance and Liam Mellows were the only two to speak on behalf of the beleaguered working class, pointing out that the Dáil had pledged itself to a workers' republic and not to the replacement of the British administration by a similarly privileged Irish ruling class. Those in favour of the Treaty argued that, in the Irish Free State, new industries would provide desperately needed employment.

Arthur Griffith pointed out that the job of the plenipotentiaries had been to negotiate the best possible deal, knowing that full independence was not an option, while Michael Collins argued that it was a stepping stone to future independence. George Russell was just one of Constance's old friends who supported the Treaty. When he told Constance, her response was succinct: 'George, you are an idiot.'

The question of the oath produced much arcane argument. Was it a question of the slave bending the knee to its masters, or an agreement between equals? The debates divided those who trusted the British prime minister and those who did not. Constance may have unwittingly weakened anti-Treaty support when, despite de Valera's opposition, she seconded a motion to adjourn the debate until after Christmas. Some believed that had the Treaty been put to a vote on 22 December, it may have been rejected. However, with fifty deputies still waiting to speak, an adjournment was inevitable.

The main avenue of publicity open to anti-Treaty Republicans was a weekly journal called *Phoblacht na hÉireann*, published in Scotland to by-pass Free State censorship. Constance, who was on the editorial committee, wrote a front page article for the 3 January 1922 issue. Under the headline 'Peace with Honour', she stated her belief that peace in Ireland was possible: 'Let the Irish people send an offer of peace to the English people, a peace that will bring confidence to Ireland, security to England, in which there will be no attempt to impose anything on the people of Ireland.'

On 3 January, when the debate resumed, Constance, in her Cumann na mBan uniform, was in more militant form. 'I rise today to oppose with all the force of my will, with all the force of my entire existence, this so-called Treaty.' She saw the oath as the biggest obstacle to accepting the Treaty – an oath to an English king when they had fought for an Irish republic would be dishonest. She would rather die than pledge an oath to King George, she said. In an emotional appeal, she also condemned what she saw as English ideals: 'love of luxury, love of wealth, love of competition, trample on your neighbours to get to the top, immorality and divorce laws'. Mere independence was not enough – she aspired to a co-operative commonwealth where workers would be equal.

She objected to southern Irish unionists sitting in a second chamber. These 'anti-Irish Irishmen' stood for 'that class of capitalists who have been more crushing, cruel and grinding on the people of the nation than any class of capitalists of whom I ever read in any other country', she declared. They had 'used the English soldiers, the English police and every institution in the country to ruin the farmer, and more especially the small farmer, and to send the people of Ireland to drift in the emigrant ships and to die of horrible disease or to sink to the bottom of the Atlantic.'

Because of her own background, she could speak out in this manner:

> Now you all know me, you know that my people came over here in Henry VIII's time, and by that bad black drop of English blood in me I know the English – that's the truth. I say it is because of that black drop in me that I know the English personally better perhaps than the people who went over on the delegation.

At this point, a pro-Treaty deputy interjected: 'Why didn't you go over?' 'Why didn't you send me?' was her riposte:

I have seen the stars, and I am not going to follow a flickering will-o'-the-wisp, and I am not going to follow any person juggling with constitutions and introducing petty, tricky ways into this Republican movement which we built up – you and not I, because I have been in jail. It has been built up and are we now going back to this tricky Parliamentarianism, because I tell you this document is nothing else.

While Ireland is not free, I remain rebel, unconverted and unconvertible ... I am pledged to the one thing – a free and independent Ireland ... a state run by the Irish people for the people. That means a government that looks after the rights of the people before the rights of property ... My idea is the Workers' Republic for which Connolly died.

Constance, who had seen too much bloodshed, claimed to have 'quite a pacific mind' and, although she was prepared to die for the cause of Ireland, she did not like to kill. Other Irish women TDs – and male deputies such as Erskine Childers – were less 'pacific'. Because all of them had either been involved in 1916, or had menfolk who had died for the cause, the 'women and Childers party', as they were dubbed, were dismissed as bitter fanatics. As the arguments became heated, many of the speakers were close to hysteria. The normally unflappable Arthur Griffith referred to Childers as 'that damned Englishman' while Constance hit Collins with a barb about his fondness for power and suggested he might like to marry an English princess.

On Saturday, 7 January 1922, a vote was taken: sixty-four for the Treaty, fifty-seven against. Arthur Griffith pointed out that the Dáil could not simply turn itself into the government of Southern Ireland and promised to keep the Republic alive until a general election. Two days later, de Valera, taking that as a vote of no confidence and a form of legal trickery, resigned his office. His re-election was immediately proposed by Kathleen Clarke and Liam Mellows, but narrowly defeated fifty-eight to sixty. De Valera did not vote; nor did Liam de Róiste, one of the few to foresee the impending disaster: 'I refuse to plunge my country into fratricide.'

Ever the realist, Michael Collins made an appeal for co-operation between the two sides, pointing out that 'when countries change from peace to war or war to peace, there are always elements that make for disorder and that make for chaos'. As he spoke, he held out his hand to de Valera. Mary MacSwiney intervened, spitting out her belief that there could be no union between the Irish Republic and the 'so-called Free State'. The moment passed and civil war became almost inevitable.

On 10 January, during a debate on Michael Collins's motion that Arthur Griffith be appointed president of the provisional government, de Valera and his followers walked out, refusing to vote. A tirade of insults followed, Collins calling them deserters and Constance responding by calling those who remained 'Lloyd Georgists', oath-breakers and cowards. The Republic she had fought for was no more. Though disappointed by the result of the vote, Constance was concerned that the walk-out would cause a split. In December 1921, she had expressed her understanding and sympathy for the delegates although she did not agree with them; she hoped they could all work together for the good of Ireland. After the Treaty was accepted, she stressed that order and peace were needed; disruption and disagreement would have serious consequences. These conciliatory words of hers are often unacknowledged.

When all had calmed down, the sixty-one deputies remaining voted unanimously for Griffith as their new president. He then proposed six cabinet ministers: Collins, finance; Gavan Duffy, foreign affairs; Duggan, home affairs; Cosgrave, local government, and Richard Mulcahy, who took over from Cathal Brugha in defence. Joseph McGrath succeeded Constance as Minster for Labour. Mulcahy, an IRA general, assured the assembly that the IRA, which two years earlier had placed itself voluntarily under the control of the Dáil, would remain the army of the Irish Republic. As it turned out, the army was soon split into pro-Treaty and anti-Treaty factions, with most of the headquarters staff in favour of the Treaty and many influential commandants on the anti-Treaty side. On 14 January, the parliament of Southern Ireland was convened by Arthur Griffith. Anti-Treaty deputies ignored the occasion. A provisional government was elected and, on 16 January, Michael Collins, as chairman, formally took over the administration of the country from the British in a ceremony at Dublin Castle.

Winston Churchill, in the colonial office, became chairman of the Cabinet Committee on Irish Affairs and the evacuation of the hated Auxiliaries and Black and Tans, along with regular British army personnel, began at once. The Royal Irish Constabulary was disbanded.

Hundreds of untried prisoners were released from detention camps and nearly 400 prisoners in British jails were given an amnesty.

On 21 January, members of the now disastrously divided Dáil met at an Irish Race Congress in Paris, planned for over a year with the aim of supporting Ireland's struggle for independence and promoting Irish trade. Representatives of seventeen countries were attending. Relations between the Republicans and the Free Staters were so poor that they travelled separately. In Paris, an exhibition of Irish art, as well as a series of concerts and lectures, began. Among the speakers were Jack B. Yeats on painting, W.B. Yeats on lyrics and plays, Douglas Hyde on the Gaelic League and Eoin MacNeill on history. Constance, Mary MacSwiney and Éamon de Valera were the Republican delegates to the congress and 'Hymn on the Battlefield', written by Constance, proved a favourite at one of the concerts. Attempts by Robert Brennan, who had organised the exhibition, to persuade the two factions to put on a united face proved fruitless. The grand ideals of the Easter Rising and equal rights for all seemed far away.

At the Sinn Féin *ard fheis* in the Mansion House on 2 February, presided over by de Valera, it was agreed to hold off elections for three months to allow a constitution, then being drafted, to be presented to the membership. Cumann na mBan had held a demonstration outside the Mansion House when the first meeting of the provisional government took place; it had become the first national body to reject the Treaty, voting twenty-four to two on a motion put forward by Constance. Members began snatching the tricolour away when it appeared on pro-Treaty platforms. A special convention was convened for 5 February to allow the overall membership to have its say; 419 voted to reject the Treaty; sixty-three were for it. Constance was re-elected president and the six women members of the Dáil all spoke strongly against the Treaty. Some prominent members supported the Treaty, among them Jenny Wyse Power, Louise Gavan Duffy, Min Ryan and Phyllis Ryan. These women, along with Alice Stopford Green, Alice Spring Rice and Griffith's wife Maud, left Cumann na mBan and founded Cumann na Saoirse.

The anti-Treaty women turned out in force for an enomous Republican demonstration in Sackville Street with speakers spread over three platforms. De Valera spoke on all three; Constance also spoke. Meetings, demonstrations and speeches followed all over the country as the hardline Republicans explained their opposition to the Treaty.

Around this time, Constance spent several weeks in London staying with Eva and Esther. She addressed meetings in London and in the Midlands, arguing the Republican case.

In Munster, the first skirmishes in what would become a bitterly fought civil war took place. Constance's native Sligo was not immune and, in February 1922, Josslyn was kidnapped from his office at Lissadell. Elsewhere, eight IRA men, who claimed that they had been on their way to a football match, were to be hanged in Derry for the deaths of two Belfast prison warders. In retaliation, the IRA rounded up a number of prominent Protestants as hostages, among them Josslyn, whose photograph was published in the *Daily Sketch* with a caption describing him as 'the brother of Countess Markievic [sic]'. Josslyn was taken by gunmen in uniform to a cottage on a side road near Grange where, with a Major Eccles, he spent the day. In the evening, the pair were released after word came through that the prisoners had been reprieved following an appeal to Sir James Craig, who had succeeded Edward Carson as leader of the Ulster Unionist Party in February 1921. Around this period, letters to Lissadell were often opened before delivery and marked 'Censored by the IRA'.

The provisional government met on 28 February and again on 1 and 2 March for three sessions. In his opening statement, Arthur Griffith said that the Belfast boycott had been discontinued and pointed out that every minister was working to see that the provisional government worked in harmony with Dáil Éireann, which would not meet until 8 June. Many activists were members of both bodies in a particularly confusing period of Irish history. Kate O'Callaghan brought up the question of giving votes to women between the ages of twenty-one and thirty so that they might vote in the June election. Her motion was seconded by Joseph MacDonagh. Updating the register would also give the vote to young men who had turned twenty-one since the previous register, many of them IRA members and anti-Treaty supporters.

On 2 March, Constance spoke, remembering her early days with the Sligo Women's Suffrage Society:

> That was my first bite you might say at the apple of freedom and soon I got on to the other freedoms, freedom to be a nation, freedom to the workers ... I have worked in Ireland, I have even

worked in England, to help the women to obtain their freedom ... It is one of the crying wrongs of the world that women, because of their sex, should be disbarred from any position or any right that their brains entitle them to hold.

She had never been happy about women's passive attitudes to public life:

There has been less physical restraint on the actions on women in Ireland than in any other country, but mentally the restrictions seem to me to be very oppressive. It is hard to understand why they took so little interest in politics as a sex, when you consider that both Catholics and Dissenters (men) laboured under all their disabilities and yet remained politicians.

As a member of the privileged class, however reluctant, she did not always grasp the problems facing ordinary women in a changing society.

Griffith saw the motion as a trick to prevent the proposed election and, while he agreed that the register of voters was hopelessly out of date, he argued that any revision must wait until after the election. He pointed to his own unwavering support for women's franchise. Constance was not placated. She accused Griffith of acting like the English parties who supported women's suffrage when it suited them. For her part, she was speaking on behalf of young women whom she counted in every way as her superiors. They had high ideals, and the education that had been denied her. They had proved their valour during the years of terror, which had dragged them out of their shells more effectively than years of work in franchise societies. She appealed to the men of the IRA to see that justice was done to 'these young women and young girls who took a man's part in the Terror'. If women were good enough to fight, they were good enough to vote. Even de Valera supported the motion saying, 'I, for one, would like to see this Dáil fulfil the pledges that were given to the women of Ireland by the men of Easter Week.' Despite his words, the motion was defeated forty-seven to thirty-eight.

Constance, in a letter to Eva, expressed her disillusionment, pointing out that women wanted to vote so they could have their say on the Treaty and that they now found their position 'humiliating'. The register was 'a farce' and Griffith clearly feared that if the register was revised, the Treaty would be beaten. She added: 'Things are awful here. There are more people being killed weekly than before the truce.' It was around this time that P.S. O'Hegarty launched his vicious attack on 'The Furies', the title he used for the women then active in politics who had lost loved ones during 1916 and its aftermath. He argued that with women in power there would be no peace.

On 26 March, a convention of the IRA took place and, although it was banned by the provisional government, anti-Treaty members attended, with Liam O'Leary named chief of staff of the IRA's military council. Although they were firmly anti-Treaty and some 4,000 boys had moved up from the Fianna to the army in the previous two years, the Fianna decided to go its own way. In January 1921, a composite council consisting of three Irish Volunteers and three Fianna had been established. Membership was variously estimated between 17,000 and 26,000, most aged between fourteen and sixteen. After the truce in the autumn of 1921, a training camp was established at Loughlinstown on the road between Dublin and Bray. At an Easter Sunday *ard fheis*, Constance was unanimously re-elected Fianna chief in her absence.

That spring, Constance was chosen by de Valera for a tour of the USA; a Free State delegation had already travelled across the Atlantic and their views needed a counterbalance. On 1 April 1922, she sailed from Southampton on the *Aquitania* with Kathleen Barry, sister of Kevin. When they arrived at the quarantine station in American waters, Constance became the centre of attention when fifty journalists boarded the *Aquitania*. Writing to Eva, she said she found ships rather like jail: 'small stuffy cabin and crowds of people around you that you don't want'. She thought it awful not to be at home in Ireland, where the difficulties ahead were 'colossal'. 'I sometimes wonder if the rank and file will ever trust a leader again. I wouldn't be a bit surprised if the army, or some of it, started out doing things on its own.' She found comfort in de Valera 'the one, strong, personal influence in the country', who, she believed, had always used that influence for unity, toleration and sanity. He could turn people's minds from vengeance to higher matters. She thought him too noble to understand crooks.

When they arrived at the Cunard Pier in New York on 7 April, they were greeted by Father O'Flanagan, Austin Stack and J.J. 'Sceilg' O'Kelly, editor of the *Catholic Bulletin* and president of the Gaelic League, as well as a crowd of sympathisers. Her mission, she told the waiting press, was 'to put the truth before the friends of Ireland in the United States'.

Constance was to discover that opinion on the Treaty was as divided in the USA as it was in Ireland. While she received an enthusiastic reception in some places, in others she was excoriated as a communist. *Gaelic American* criticised de Valera's speeches and wrote nothing of Constance's tour. During her five days in New York, she attended meetings, held interviews and met supporters, firstly in Lexington, then Newark and finally Jersey City, as well as holding a secret meeting with Clan na Gael. She took a day off to visit Jim Larkin in Sing Sing Prison in upstate New York, where the warden gave her a tour of the penitentiary. She was impressed, finding it much superior to any British or Irish jail she had known. She loved American food and coffee but was not so impressed by central heating. She developed an addiction to chewing gum, considered very unladylike at the time.

Next stop was Philadelphia, where the delegation arrived to an enthusiastic reception at Broad Street station on Good Friday afternoon. The following day, Constance was shown the historic buildings of the city, including Valley Forge, where she achieved her ambition 'to walk in the hallowed footsteps of Washington'. She was thrilled to meet up with 'Chicago May' Sharpe, her old comrade from Aylesbury jail.

On Easter Sunday, she and Barry were escorted to mass by Irish-American Volunteers in uniform and a brass band. After a long lunch, they went to the Irish American Club. She made a speech assuring her audience that the anti-Treaty Republican movement did not consist merely of fanatical followers of de Valera, but existed out of a profound conviction that Ireland 'must and will be a Republic'. It would need moral and financial support, she added. Later in the day, they were accompanied by a bodyguard of 200 Volunteers to a meeting at the Academy of Music, where Austin Stack and J.J. O'Kelly shared the platform and Joe McGarrity chaired. While the audience cheered every mention of de Valera and booed references to Lloyd George, it showed a charitable attitude to Griffith and Collins; relations between the Free Staters and the Republicans were still cordial.

They travelled on to Detroit, followed by a quick trip across the border to Windsor in Canada. In Akron, Ohio, they received a cooler reception;

a local newspaper had published a leader praising the Free Staters who had visited a few days earlier. Cleveland, St Paul-Minneapolis and Butte, Montana, followed – all of them Irish-American strongholds. Although their arrival in Anaconda was delayed by a snowstorm, Constance was greeted by a standing ovation. In Butte, they were met by the Pearse and Connolly fife and drum band at the head of a large delegation of sympathisers. 'Butte was one of the places that stand out for its reception for they met us with a band and an army. All Sligo seemed to be there!'

She was shocked to see how the town's copper miners lived and she insisted on seeing how the men worked. 'I saw a man drilling the copper ore without the water appliance to keep the dust down and breathing in copper dust eight mortal hours every day. They told us few men live to be old in Butte, Montana.' On Sunday, 30 April, there was a meeting in Butte High School.

Next Constance travelled across the Rockies and the wastelands of Montana to the Pacific seaboard cities of Seattle and Portland. In Seattle, she was met by her friend and comrade Lily Kempson, a veteran of the Easter Rising, who had settled in the United States. The small party travelled to Portland and then on to San Francisco arriving on 6 May to be greeted by a deputation dressed in ancient Gaelic dress. While in San Francisco, the delegation received news of the forthcoming 'pact' election. After visiting Los Angeles, where Tom Clarke's son Daly was waiting, it was time to head back to the east coast with a spectacular five-day railway journey weaving around mountains and crossing ravines. By 14 May, Constance was back in the town of Springfield, Massachusetts.

Almost everywhere she went, Constance addressed enthusiastic crowds and met old friends. She repeated her antagonistic view of the Irish Free State – it was not Irish, not free and not a state, she said. After her meeting in Springfield, she spent a day with J.J. Hearn in nearby Westfield, Massachusetts, sitting under an apple tree in blossom, revelling in the lilac and discovering a bird's nest. On a child's blackboard, she saw a slogan written in Irish: 'Colmcille's prophecy full of hope for Ireland' signed by Liam Mellows. She liked what she saw of American towns and houses – they were well kept, with good gardens, no walls to separate them and the wonder of built-in wardrobes. In

Cincinnati, she found another beautiful garden, full of flowering shrubs and roses, at the home of A.J. Castellini, whom she had met at the 1922 Irish Race Congress in Paris.

A visit to Chicago followed and, after that, a farewell week in Boston, beginning with an address to members of Cumann na mBan and followed by meetings in New Bedford, Lynn, Norwood, Lawrence, Full River, Worcester and in the Maple Street playgrounds, Holyoke. Constance's journey brought home to her the immensity of the USA with its diverse landscapes and climatic conditions. She had started out in the east in early spring, shivered in Montana's winter snowstorms and enjoyed summery conditions in San Francisco. In Los Angeles, she marvelled at the palm trees and orange groves and, in Arizona, she was awestruck by the barren desert.

On 22 May, Constance was cheered for six minutes by a crowd of five thousand at a meeting in New York's Madison Square Garden. She made a powerful speech denouncing the Treaty as 'nothing but a surrender'. Her companion, Kathleen Barry, recalled her twin personality: the private Constance who was 'thoughtful, interesting and interested in the young' and the public Constance who was confident, extrovert and charismatic. The crowds loved her and she was careful – as always – to tailor her speeches to her audience. On 30 May, she and Kathleen Barry set sail for home on the Cunard Line's *Berengaria*.

While in St Paul, Constance had begun a long letter to Staskou. She explained that she had not written before because she was afraid of compromising him. She had sent him many messages through Eva, who in turn, had passed his messages on to her. 'You know I've had a pretty stiff time of it, about three years and a half, and some of it was awful.'

She referred to the time he was held captive. 'I did what I could to help you and I think that some of the people whom I got to intercede for you may have been a little help.'

She longed to see him again and worried about Casimir:

You were always as dear to me as if you had been my own son. Also dear Casi, I hate to think of him having to work on a job. Of course, we are all frightfully poor now, for money won't buy anything. I wonder if he got the money I sent him from Ireland. He never wrote, at least I never got the letter.

She revealed her growing weariness with politics: 'what I begin to believe is that all governments are the same, and that men in power use that power for themselves and are absolutely unscrupulous in their dealings with those who disagree with them'. She ended the letter 'Now goodbye darling boy and much love from your loving Mother.'

During this trip, Constance spoke to Kathleen Barry about her daughter Maeve, whom she had not seen since before her imprisonment in Cork. Despite having little money, she bought many presents for her, including Hudson Bay furs in Seattle. When the two women finally reached London, Constance spent her first day with Eva, returning to her hotel at about ten o'clock. Kathleen went to bed but was interrupted by a housemaid who told her that a woman wanted to see Constance, but that there was no answer from her room. Behind the chambermaid was a tall young woman who said she must see Constance. It was Maeve, who had heard through Eva that her mother was in London. When Barry suggested that she look downstairs, Maeve confessed that she was not sure that she would recognise her mother. Armed with a description from Barry, she went downstairs but was soon back unsure about whether the woman she had seen having coffee with two friends was indeed her mother. It was.

In Ireland, having two rival armies in one country was promising nothing but trouble; de Valera and Collins urged moderation and did their best to recreate the unity the rebels had known when opposing the British during the Anglo-Irish War. Unfortunately, fighting men thrown up in a crisis rarely have the patience and the negotiating skills necessary for a peaceful life. Most ominously, Ireland had no tradition of peaceful opposition to fall back on; disagreements were traditionally resolved by violence and the hard men admired. With the election dividing the nation, pistols were cleaned and rifles retrieved from lofts and attics. The country would again fall under the shadow of the gunmen.

CHAPTER SEVENTEEN

Anarchy is Loosed

On 14 April, the anti-Treaty Republicans occupied the Four Courts building on Dublin's quays in defiance of the provisional government. Smaller groups moved into other buildings, including the Rotunda Hospital, and Fowler Hall on Rutland (now Parnell) Square, which was then an Orange lodge. The aim was to force a new confrontation with the British that might reunite the two Sinn Féin factions.

Although Griffith wanted to quell this rebel act immediately, Collins stood back, wary of plunging the country into civil war. A week later, at midnight on 20 April, anti-Treaty fighters attacked pro-Treaty troops stationed at the provisional government headquarters in Merrion Square. They also attacked the Bank of Ireland on College Green, the telephone exchange in Temple Bar, and City Hall. Three people were wounded.

In early May, the anti-Treaty Republicans took over the centre of Kilkenny, with provisional government troops sent from Dublin to dislodge them. While the country slid towards civil war, an uneasy truce between the two sides was announced in the Dáil. Towards the end of the month, de Valera and Collins presented a plan for a national coalition panel that would skirt around the tricky issue of the Treaty and form a government after the forthcoming election. The panel would represent pro- and anti-Treaty groupings, with numbers depending on the relative strengths of the groups.

Constance attended her last Dáil meeting on 8 June. A photograph of the time shows her pushing her bicycle on a visit to her constituency; she is surrounded by children and looks thin and haggard. On the eve of the election on 16 June, she spoke at a rally on York Street, declaring that Sinn Féin wanted law and order in Ireland, as well as food for the starving and work for the unemployed. For the house of 128 members, ninety-four Sinn Féin candidates were returned. Of these, fifty-eight were pro-Treaty and thirty-six anti-Treaty. The Labour Party, one of the parties urging unity, returned seventeen members, the Farmers' Party seven, Unionists (Trinity College) four, and Independents six. The four South Dublin City deputies consisted of two pro-Treaty members from the agreed panel, as well as one Labour and one Independent deputy. Pro-treaty Sinn Féin won 239,193 votes, compared to 133,864 for anti-Treaty Sinn Féin, with a further 247,226 voting for other parties. Constance lost her seat, as did Margaret Pearse, Ada English and Kathleen Clarke. Kate O'Callaghan in Limerick and Mary MacSwiney in Cork were both elected in strong anti-Treaty areas. As far as the British were concerned, the election results endorsed the Treaty and it was absolutely clear that the people wanted peace. However, the anti-Treaty Republicans were not prepared to listen.

On 22 June, Field Marshal Sir Henry Wilson was shot dead on his doorstep in London by two members of the IRA's London battalion. Wilson, an Irishman born in Longford, had been military adviser to the six-county government and was blamed by nationalists – and Michael Collins – for the reign of terror against Catholics in the North. His murder provoked a wave of anti-Irish fury, and Winston Churchill made it clear that if the situation worsened, Britain would take whatever steps necessary to safeguard its interests in Ireland.

On 26 June, a motor car agency in Dublin's Baggot Street had sixteen of its cars 'requisitioned' by anti-Treaty Republican troops as part of the 'Belfast Boycott'. The officer in charge, Leo Henderson, was arrested by pro-Treaty troops and, in reprisal, pro-Treaty deputy chief of staff J.J. 'Ginger' O'Connell was kidnapped and held by the anti-Treaty troops in the Four Courts. This was the final blow for Churchill, who warned Michael Collins that if he did not act against the anti-Treaty Republicans, Britain would be forced to. Collins reluctantly ordered an attack on the Four Courts after an ultimatum to surrender was ignored.

On 28 June, after a day of rumour, the citizens of Dublin awoke to the boom of heavy guns; the Civil War had begun. Constance, some three miles away in Rathgar, recognised it for what it was – an attack on the Four Courts. The bombardment of the beautiful Gandon building continued, first using two and then four eighteen-pounder field guns. Spectators lined both sides of the Liffey to watch 'the show'. On the second day of the battle, Free State troops stormed the east wing of the building, taking over thirty prisoners. Three were killed and fourteen wounded. After two days of constant pummelling, fires were raging and the west wing of the building was shaken by a powerful explosion when the fires spread to the munitions stored in the Public Records Office. Priceless records dating back to the Middle Ages went up in smoke. In the mid-afternoon of 30 June, men in the garrison surrendered after throwing their weapons into the fire.

Fighting continued on Sackville Street, where members of the anti-Treaty Dublin Brigade, led by Oscar Traynor, had occupied a number of buildings on the east side of the street. Cathal Brugha, Éamon de Valera, Austin Stack and Robert Barton were among those reporting for duty, while Constance was one of several Cumann na mBan members mobilised. She would spend time at Barry's Hotel on Great Denmark Street with John Hanratty and at the Hammam Hotel in Sackville Street. From Whelan's Hotel on Eccles Street, she organised a group of Red Cross nurses to go to the west, among them the novelist Annie M.P. Smithson. The plan was to hold out for as long as possible and give the Irish Republican Army in the provinces time to mobilise. Since Easter Week, the Republicans had learned much about street fighting and they could not be cornered easily.

Some seventy men and thirty women were mobilised in the block from the Hammam Hotel to the Gresham Hotel on Sackville Street. Across the road, on Henry Street, was a sniping post on the rooftops, manned by two or three riflemen. One of those riflemen described his experiences in a 1960 newspaper article:

> It made my position in the shelter of the cornice as dangerous a one as you could find. I was due for relief and I wasn't sorry for that. But when my relief came, who was it but Madame. Played out as I was after two or three hours up there under continuous fire, I didn't like the idea of a woman taking over that position. But Madame just waved me to one side with that imperious air she could put on when she wanted to have her own way. She slipped

into what little shelter there was, carrying with her an automatic Parabellum pistol – the kind we used to call a Peter the Painter. I couldn't rightly say how long she was up there, for I was so tired that I drowsed off to sleep. But when I woke up, the first thing I noticed was something different in the sound of the firing. The steady, continuous rattle of fire that I had learned to pick out from the sound of rifle and machine gun fire up and down the street had ceased; the sniper's post in Henry Street was silent.

On 5 July, a group of twenty, including three women nurses, were ushered out of the burning Hammam Hotel by Cathal Brugha. Among the last to go were Constance and some of the other women who walked out the back door of the hotel. Brugha went out the front with a gun blazing from each hand. He was mown down and died two days later from blood loss after a fatal shot to the thigh. It was the end of eight days of fighting in Dublin's city centre with over sixty killed, about 300 wounded and a large part of the city in ruins.

Two days later, on 7 July, Churchill sent Collins a message of congratulations. The fighting was not over and, within months, some of the bravest and the best were dead: Collins, Mellows, Childers, Griffith. On 30 July, Harry Boland was mortally wounded in Skerries by Free State troops who had come to arrest him. He died on 2 August. Boland had been one of Collins's closest allies but, when he changed sides, was shot on the orders of his friend, according to a statement by Constance in the semi-underground *Fenian* bulletin that was published from July to October of that year. Cumann na mBan provided the guard of honour at his funeral.

On 12 August, Arthur Griffith, aged fifty, died in a Dublin hospital of a cerebral haemorrhage, paying the ultimate price for the strain of the previous decade. Ten days later, on 22 August 1922, Michael Collins was ambushed and shot dead at Béal na Bláth in County Cork by anti-Treaty fighters. Denis 'Sonny' O'Brien, a former Royal Irish Constabulary man, was believed to have fired the fatal shot. Collins was regarded by many as the only politician capable of restraining a government that would rely increasingly on a regime of legalised terror.

The newly elected third Dáil and provisional government finally met in Leinster House on 9 September at the main lecture theatre attached to

Leinster House, then owned by the Royal Dublin Society; the building was bought outright from the Royal Dublin Society in 1924. Whether the new Dáil was a republican parliament or a crown assembly was not at all clear. Republicans elected in June did not attend, with the exception of Laurence Ginnell. When he stepped forward to sign the roll, he queried under whose authority they were meeting. After several unsuccessful attempts to get his question answered, he was forcibly ejected from the meeting. William Cosgrave was elected president in succession to Griffith. The constitution was debated and enacted.

With anti-Treaty Republicans under constant threat of arrest, Constance was on the run, staying with a succession of friends. She wrote articles for pro-Republican publications in the USA and helped Maud Gonne MacBride with the Women's Prisoners' Defence League. She was in Carrick-on-Suir in March and April where workers' co-operatives had taken over creameries and factories. Later that summer, she visited Clonmel, delivering an address from the steps of the town hall. Carrick-on-Suir was taken over by the Free State Army on 2 August and Clonmel on 8/9 August.

In the late summer and early autumn of 1922, Constance produced an anti-Treaty paper, writing most of the copy, drawing the political cartoons and printing it off on a Roneo duplicator until the machine was seized in a raid. In September, following the ambush on Collins, carrying a weapon had become an offence punishable by death under the Public Safety Act. Martial law and military courts became a reality on 15 October 1922. 'If murderous attacks take place, those who persist in those murderous attacks must learn that they have got to pay the penalty for them,' William Cosgrave told the Dáil, adding that, although he had always objected to the death penalty, this was a last resort in an effort to restore order to the country. General Mulcahy argued that the act would help regulate the anarchy and unlawful executions taking place on both sides of the divide. The Labour Party's Thomas Johnson opposed the Bill, likening it to a military dictatorship.

A total of eighty-one men would be executed by the Irish Free State, with Erskine Childers on 24 November the most notorious case. His crime was to possess a small pistol given to him by Michael Collins. He was followed four weeks later by the four men who had surrendered the Four Courts and had been held since then without trial in Mountjoy:

Liam Mellows and Rory O'Connor, both former Fianna boys, along with Joseph McKelvey and Richard Barrett. Since their crimes had been committed before the October proclamation, the executions were thought to be a response to the murder of Seán Hales and the serious injury to Pádraic Ó Máille, both of them Dáil deputies, on 7 December. Maud Gonne MacBride and the Women's Prisoners' Defence League organised a protest against the executions outside the house of the Minister for Defence, Richard Mulcahy. The Catholic hierarchy decided to excommunicate all Republicans who 'in the absence of any legitimate authority to justify it [were carrying out] a system of murder'.

Saorstát na hÉireann, the Irish Free State, was proclaimed on 6 December 1922, the first anniversary of the Treaty signing in London. William T. Cosgrave was elected president and the veteran Irish nationalist Tim Healy was named Ireland's first Governor General. When Cosgrave issued his list of thirty senators, it included W.B. Yeats, Sir Horace Plunkett, Oliver St John Gogarty and Jenny Wyse Power. Among the thirty elected senators were Alice Stopford Green and Colonel Maurice Moore. On 7 December, the Northern Ireland parliament voted to remain part of the United Kingdom.

On 27 December, Æ's open letter to Irish republicans was published in the *Irish Times*. While admitting his fondness for the 'underman' in a conflict, he appealed to the republicans to change their thinking.

> No ideal, however noble in itself, can remain for long lovable or desirable in the minds of men while it is associated with deeds such as have been done in recent years in Ireland ... I do not like to think of you that the only service you can render Ireland is to shed blood on its behalf.

His words were ignored. The homes of senators became targets, with the houses of Sir Horace Plunkett in Foxrock and St John Gogarty in Connemara among the thirty-seven burned to the ground. In the Curragh, seven 'Irregulars' were executed in one day and, in February 1923, the father of Kevin O'Higgins, the hard-line Minister for Justice, was shot dead in his home in Stradbally, County Laois, by anti-Treaty republicans. Constance made no mention of this brutality in a letter to Staskou, writing only of her efforts to send him money and to find a job.

In January 1923, Constance, accompanied by May Coghlan, took a ten-week break from the unrelenting horror of the Civil War with a trip to Scotland, followed by a visit to Eva in London. 'The Red Countess' was fully occupied addressing meetings, visiting Sinn Féin clubs and attending receptions and fêtes. She averaged two meetings every Sunday and two or three during the week, outlining the appalling treachery and tragedy of the Treaty and its aftermath. The British Special Branch followed her movements closely but did not attempt an arrest, possibly because the meetings did not attract big numbers. The month she spent with Eva in London from mid-March was the first extended stretch of time the sisters had spent together in years. She enjoyed walking streets that were full of memories for her, passing the homes of old friends, the church where she had been married and other familiar haunts, including the House of Commons.

Phobhlacht na hÉireann, promoting the anti-Treaty argument, had ceased publication in January 1923 and was immediately succeeded by *Eire, the Irish Nation*, published in Glasgow until April and after that in Manchester. Constance was always ready to contribute and wrote several articles under the general heading of 'My Experiences of Easter Week', referring mainly to the bravery of others. In April, on the anniversary of Easter 1916, she was in Dumbarton, Scotland, where she moved her audience to tears with her description of the sufferings inflicted on republican prisoners by Free State jailers. She seemed relieved to be away from Ireland and the threat of ending up in prison again. However, she had told de Valera that she was willing to do 'anything' he ordered her to do either there or in Ireland.

Constance argued that the conflict in Ireland pitted the ideals of an ancient Gaelic civilisation against the 'modern, moral anarchy of industrialism'.

> The Gaelic civilisation was founded on ideas of co-operation and de-centralisation, and the ambitions and talents of the people were directed towards learning art, beauty and holiness which alone can bring happiness and a lasting greatness to a people, and away from the terrible competition for luxury which had led to all the miseries and vices of an industrial nation.

For Constance, the new senate was an excuse to entrench the old Anglo-Irish landlord class in the new administration, while many Castle officials were finding jobs in a free state, which, in its structure and administration, mirrored what had gone before. While this was disappointing for a champion of the working class like herself, Constance would prove a pragmatist, unlike the dwindling rump of hard-liners.

During this time, the implacably republican Mary MacSwiney, along with Kate O'Callaghan, Dorothy Macardle, Máire Comerford and Sighle Humphreys, niece of The O'Rahilly, were on hunger strike in Kilmainham Gaol, demanding better conditions. On the nineteenth day of MacSwiney and O'Callaghan's hunger strike, the governor decided to move eighty-one prisoners to the North Dublin Union in Grangegorman, close to the Broadstone railway station. It took five hours to remove them forcibly. The next day, MacSwiney was released, with her aim of becoming a martyr like her brother thwarted.

By April, Constance was back in Dublin and she travelled to Clonmel where, on 10 April, she and de Valera narrowly escaped when a meeting of Republicans to discuss ending hostilities was ambushed by the Free State Army. Liam Lynch, the anti-Treaty army leader, was shot and captured. While the IRA could muster about 8,000 fighting men, the Irish Free State could call on an army of 38,000 and, after meeting army executives, de Valera for the Republican government and Frank Aiken (who would later become a key Fianna Fáil minister) for the Free State Army agreed to a ceasefire that would begin on 30 April 1923.

Less than a month later, on 24 May 1923, the Civil War ended with weapons and arms dumped. Hundreds of lives had been lost and the cost had spiralled to about £17m. In a message to his followers, de Valera admitted that further loss of life would achieve nothing: 'seven years of intense effort have exhausted our people ... A little time and you will see them recover and rally again to the standard.' An estimated 11,316, including 250 women, were held in prison – most without trial. To keep them there, the government rushed through the Public Safety Act in June. A confident government then called an election for 27 August, expecting to get unambiguous support for the Treaty.

In 1923, mainstream politicians were paying scant attention to the curse of unemployment – they believed it was a problem to be solved by public works and support for home industries. With her eye always on the poor and downtrodden, Constance sought to combine the policies of Sinn Féin and Labour, believing it important that labour and republicans fought the same battles. Yet, in the run-up to the election of August 1923, Sinn Féin did not present any economic or social programme. In contrast, Labour came up with a moderate reformist programme, their goal a republic run on the lines of a co-operative commonwealth. While the aims of Labour mirrored those of Constance, there was one essential difference: Labour was pro-Treaty and, some even argued, pro-British.

For the election, a reorganised Sinn Féin put forward eighty-seven candidates, although most were still on the run. De Valera, in a note to Constance, had said that he had decided to take the risk of speaking on 15 August in Ennis. He was arrested and remained in solitary confinement without trial for almost a year. Of the 153 seats in the Free State parliament, the government party won sixty-three, five more than in 1922, while the Republicans won forty-four, eight more than in 1922. The Farmers' Party, representing larger landowners, took fifteen seats, one more than the Labour Party. It was the first time that women aged between twenty-one and thirty had voted. Constance regained her seat in South Dublin City, but she and other Republican representatives refused to take their seats in the new government because of the contentious oath to the king of England.

These were bleak days for radicals and idealists, with the government continuing to make arrests. The Free Staters, now called Cumann na nGael, were governing in the interests of the business community, farmers and professionals. Constance had long repudiated the wealth, status and privilege that they found important. Economic policy was conservative, aiming at fiscal rectitude and deflation, with salaries and pensions cut back and no possibility of growth. Ireland remained the poorest region in the islands of Britain and Ireland. Many were forced to emigrate, not only because there were few jobs on offer, but because employees of the new state were obliged to swear an oath of allegiance before they could take up jobs as teachers, gardaí or civil servants. Those in power blamed unemployment on indolence or the restrictive practices of trade unions; the poor were largely believed to have brought their misfortunes on themselves. Cosgrave relegated the Department of Labour, once so proudly run by Constance, to a section of the Department of Industry and Finance. Women workers were ignored and sidelined.

The new government's administrative machinery was far from Connolly and Constance's ideal of a workers' republic run on co-operative lines. The new state supported Gaelic culture and the Irish language, but socially it was extremely conservative and the influence of the Catholic Church was considerable. Women returned to the kitchen, divorce was made impossible and films and books were censored.

In September, a series of three articles written by Constance for the British Labour *Forward* publication were reprinted in pamphlet form as 'What Irish Republicans Stand For'. She dedicated the leaflet to the memory of Wolfe Tone, John Mitchel, James Fintan Lalor and James Connolly and favoured facts over polemic, outlining the achievements of the Dáil during the Black and Tan days and comparing it to the current parliament. She repeated her lifelong belief in the co-operative movement. The Free State she described as: 'devised by the British cabinet of imperialists and capitalists and accepted by their would-be counterparts in Ireland, whom they supply with money, arms, and men for the purpose of breaking up the growing movement of the Co-Operative Commonwealth of Ireland'.

She attempted to clarify what had been achieved before the Treaty:

> As, step by step, the Republican Government became the *de facto* Government of Ireland, it began slowly to reorganise the national services on more democratic and Gaelic lines. Of course, we had to go very slowly and carefully, for not only were we faced with the difficulties which invariably face the development of any country on any lines, but we faced also the fact that an enemy army was in occupation of our country and that the whole nation was individually 'on the run'.

She outlined the achievements of the Home Office under Austin Stack, in particular the justice system and the work she had promoted in the Department of Labour.

'The only sane course for Ireland is co-operation,' she wrote, pointing out how the British had attacked co-operative creameries and other enterprises as part of their policy to break the republican movement. She gave many examples of the non-co-operative nature of the new Irish government. 'We Republicans ask: why encourage the "peaceful penetration" of Ireland by English capitalists, instead of trying to develop trade and industries ourselves on co-operative lines?' She would continue to work for 'a commonwealth based on Gaelic ideals'.

Ultimately, the interned republican prisoners got maximum publicity for their cause when they resorted to the most extreme measures: the hunger strike. On 13 October, 424 republican prisoners refused food in Mountjoy Gaol. The hunger strike spread to other prisons and camps and, within two weeks, nearly 9,000 were refusing food. Many of the women prisoners were interned at the North Dublin Union. Accommodation in the building, formerly a poor house and then a Black and Tan barracks, consisted of large drafty dormitories. Bathroom facilities were primitive and the building was haunted by 'ghosts of broken-hearted paupers'. The women passed their time drilling, sewing, knitting and reading.

Constance busied herself campaigning on their behalf. Her Sligo friend, Baby Bohan, from Ballymote was one of the women interned and her worried family had sent her sister Doty to Dublin to get news. One day, Doty came across a crowd gathered around a dray. It was Constance, 'our own Sligo heroine', appealing to the crowd to go to City Hall and sign a petition for the release of the prisoners. There seemed no possible justification for detaining either the women or other republican prisoners. At the Sinn Féin *ard fheis*, the virtues of passive non-military resistance were emphasised. The policy of armed resistance was abandoned.

On 20 November, Constance was arrested while on a day's canvassing with Hanna Sheehy Skeffington and two other younger women, mostly in Constance's inner city constituency. Late in the afternoon, three detectives stepped in front of their lorry at Kevin Street and Constance was arrested and taken by car to the Bridewell, where she was held without charge. When her captors offered her tea, she refused, saying that she would join the other prisoners on hunger strike; the day of her arrest, Dennis Barry, who had gone thirty-four days without food, died in Newbridge jail. In the evening, Sheehy Skeffington and Maud Gonne MacBride visited her with offers of food and clothing, which she refused. Next stop was the North Dublin Union, where Constance heard that Baby Bohan was so ill that she had been given the last rites. Constance's hunger strike lasted for only three days and she reported that the anticipation of suffering had been the worst part. She slept most of the time and had lovely dreams. She stated, 'I was perfectly happy and had no regrets.' She painted a good deal, making dozens of watercolours.

On 23 November, after forty-one days, the hunger strike in all the prisons was called off, though not before two men had died. Constance startled her jailers by insisting on scrubbing floors, with her skirt tucked into her bloomers. She busied herself getting Baby Bohan back to full strength, cooking for her and spending hours sitting on her bed, supporting her with her own body to ease her backache. She gave her mittens to protect her shrivelled hands from the cold. After Baby was released and went back to her family in Sligo, she sent Constance a pair of black cashmere mittens.

Five weeks after her arrest, on Christmas Eve, Constance was released. She was thin and pale, but found that her rheumatism had gone, as had her stomach trouble. On one of her first public appearances after her release, she delivered the oration at the grave of the ex-Fianna chief scout Liam Mellows on the first anniversary of his death.

To judge by a letter to Eva that December, she was increasingly sceptical when it came to both religion and politics: 'For every church and every sect is but an organisation of thoughtless and well-meaning people trained in thought and controlled by juntas of priests and clergy who are doing all the things that Christ would have most disliked.' The same she believed was true of 'all public bodies and governments'. What was needed was 'some scheme by which power can be evenly distributed ... and by which the foolish and uneducated can no longer be grouped in unthinking battalions dependent on the few pushers, self-seekers and crooks, and made slaves of and exploited.' She sounded deflated: 'Everything here is very dull. The main thing is the appalling poverty that meets one everywhere ...'

During the month, 3,481 prisoners were released, including all the women. It was a false dawn. In January 1924, the Irish government issued another Public Safety Act allowing for detention without trial. Once again, republican prisoners began filling the jails.

CHAPTER EIGHTEEN

No Enemy but Time

In 1924, Irish Republicans were rebuilding their shattered organisation, with the dream of establishing an independent republic undimmed. 'We were flattened. We felt the Irish public had forgotten us. The tinted trappings of our fight were hanging like rags around us' was how Sighle Humphreys described it.

At a general meeting of Cumann na mBan in April, Constance presented a plan to continue military training while, at the same time, adapting to changing conditions. There would be lectures on historical, social and economic subjects and first aid classes, as well as monthly military and physical drilling. Irish games and the Irish language were promoted, while the co-operative movement was highlighted as a solution to the plague of unemployment. Recent events were alluded to by Constance in her presidential address. 'No-one knows when we may be attacked again or when we may see our chance to strike again. Peace is beautiful and we want peace, but we cannot shirk the fight if it is the only way to win.' She still possessed an ability to strike the right note and, as she had done at the 1921 congress, she gave the women hope. Yet Cumann na mBan was losing members; many long-time members were tired and demoralised, while others felt the call of family life or needed to earn a living.

Constance worked hard, putting in hours of canvassing at several by-elections that year. The first was in Limerick, where the republican movement was getting back on its feet. To a friend she wrote:

I never saw worse slums or met nicer people. Don't talk to me about politics, tell me how to get bread for the children was the general cry. If one could only get the people to understand that politics ought to be nothing more or less than the organisation of food, clothes, housing and transit of every unit of the nation, one would get a lot further. Also if they would only learn to watch and heckle their leaders, aye, and distrust them, fear them more than their opponents.

She wished people would read, study and make up their own minds about their lives and how to run them, 'but alas it's always their impulse to get behind some idol, let him do all the thinking for them and then be surprised when he leads them all wrong'. She never lost belief in the power of education, organisation, co-operation, honour and courage as the cornerstones of a working republic.

In the summer, her pamphlet 'James Connolly's Policy and Catholic Doctrine' was published by Sinn Féin. A priest, Dr Peter Coffey of Maynooth, had written an article on 'James Connolly's Campaign against Capitalism, in the light of Catholic Teaching' for the *Catholic Bulletin* of 1920. In her article, Constance defends Connolly and makes a strenuous attempt to reconcile her socialism with the Catholicism she had adopted, referring to Pope Leo XIII's 1891 *Encyclical on the Condition of the Working Class* as well as to Dr Coffey's article.

In the first half of the closely written 45-page document, she outlines Connolly's socialism and concludes that 'state socialism', with all citizens as employees of the state, would be condemned by both Connolly and Pope Leo XIII. Regarding what Dr Coffey had called Connolly's 'anti-clericalism' she argues that Connolly had been misunderstood. Although the Catholic Church might recognise a de facto state and social order, individual citizens could still fight for a better world, without being any less Catholic.

In the second half of the pamphlet on 'Connolly's Programmes and Catholic Doctrine', Constance begins by considering his 1896 programme for the Irish Socialist Republican Party. She argues that Connolly's fundamental idea of Ireland as an independent republic based on Gaelic ideals never changed, although he reconsidered the tactics by which this could be achieved depending on circumstances. She examines his ideas on education and on state banks and the relationship between his nationalism and internationalism. To Connolly, Home Rule meant accepting capitalism and imperialism. She points out that the clergy who had attacked the republic had said nothing about the 'treacherous and unprovoked' attack on the Four Courts, and had ignored the cruel treatment of prisoners. She concludes with the personal belief that the writings left by Connolly would always be Gospel for his friends and those who fought under his leadership. 'The writings he has left us are the marching orders of a risen people.'

Casimir came to London from Poland that year on a diplomatic mission and travelled on to Dublin, the city he had left eleven years previously. In Warsaw, his plays were keeping him solvent. Constance was excited and full of joy at the news that her estranged husband was coming. Although she had aged greatly since he had last seen her, he found that, in many ways, she was the same old Con, full of energy and optimism. Dublin, in the middle of an economic depression, had changed and he found the post-war city dreary and most of his friends scattered. Although Constance usually scraped by, she worried about her friends who were not so well off, as she wrote to Staskou after Casimir had returned to Poland. 'All the small businesses here are heading for ruin and the farmers are in a bad way ... Taxes are awful and food prices are daily rising and rents are wicked.'

Constance continued to speak whenever she was asked for Sinn Féin, Cumann na mBan, the Women's Prisoners' Defence League, the Fianna and the labour movement. In June, the remaining political prisoners were finally released, although the government was determined to stick to a strict law-and-order policy. A few weeks later, Constance went with de Valera to Sligo for a monster meeting to celebrate his release after almost eleven months in Kilmainham Gaol. He was the last prisoner ever held in that grim place. In her native county, Constance had a happy reunion with the Bohan sisters and, at a *céilí* in the town hall, she danced the night away. Now a local celebrity, she threw out the ball at a football match between ex-internees of Dublin and Sligo.

In Dublin, Constance presided over the Cumann na mBan convention on 3 November. A day later, she attended the Sinn Féin *ard fheis* where, in his absence, 1,300 delegates re-elected de Valera as president; he had been detained in Belfast after crossing the border to speak in Derry. In 1925, Sinn Féin won only two of the nine seats at the seven by-elections held on 11 March. Oscar Traynor was elected in North Dublin and

Samuel Holt took one of two vacant seats in Sligo-Leitrim. Constance had spoken in support of Holt at a rally in Ballymote.

Casimir's visit had revived Constance's interest in the theatre and, in September 1925, she helped establish the Republican Players Dramatic Society. Within a year, the players had produced a dozen plays, including two one-act plays she had written. *The Invincible Mother* was set in Kilmainham Gaol in the 1880s and, along with *Blood Money*, set in 1798, it was performed at the Abbey on 1 March 1925. She had begun a full-length play, *Broken Dreams*, based on her own disillusioning experiences during the Black and Tan war and scribbled at it in a copy book whenever she had a spare few minutes.

Broken Dreams tells the story of 'an incident in the Black and Tan war'. The heroine, Eileen O'Rourke, a Cumann na mBan officer, is tall and slim, with short brown hair and a striking face. In manner she is like a young boy and she wears practical clothes – just as Constance did. Her troubles begin when her cruel drunkard husband, Seamus, jealous of Eileen's friendship with another man called Eamon, is shot dead after a drunken row with Eileen. Eileen is blamed for the killing because she is known to be a good shot. After various adventures, she discovers that Seamus had been an informer. Standing by is Eamon, who remains honourable throughout. In his curtain speech he says: 'God only gives happiness to those who give all. It is only where there is no self, there is God.' The play was was never performed during Constance's life; it had its first performance on 11 December 1927.

Mary Colum described meeting her old friend around this period and the portrait was unflinching: 'she was like an extinct volcano, her former violent self reduced to something burnt out ... haggard and old, dressed in ancient demoded clothes'. The long years of fighting, imprisonment and bad food had worn her down and she was obviously failing, with the old fire and eagerness gone from her eyes. In Colum's view, Constance was a disappointed woman. 'What she had fought for had not really come into being; maybe nothing on earth could have brought it into being so romantic and heroic was it.'

The delight of her life in those later years was her car – a battered 'Tin Lizzie' she had picked up at an army sale. As often as she could, she would pack paints, food, children, friends and dog into the car and head for the countryside. Constance in her car – or indeed under her car – became as familiar a sight as Constance on her bicycle in earlier days. Because it broke down frequently, she never travelled without a ball of twine for emergency repairs. Máire Nic Shiubhlaigh remembered Constance's daredevil driving: 'She used to drive this [car] around the city as fast as it would go. Its joints rattled and clanked but Madame sat at the wheel, every bit of her enjoying it.'

At the Coghlan's, she had free run of the garden, which was her other delight, especially after a long day of meetings. She saw her mother when she came to Dublin for shopping, while her daughter Maeve, who had grown tall and pretty, was a joy to her.

In June 1925, she was co-opted to the Rathmines and Rathgar Urban District Council. As a member of the Housing, Public Health, Old Age Pensions and Child Welfare committees, she dealt with everything from keeping pigs in the backyard to job discrimination. She would stand at the back wall, a restless presence, shouting 'Ahoy there, you!' to anyone whose attention she wished to attract. Her presence ensured that many of the meetings were stormy; she fought against the need for taking an oath before securing a job and demanded to know why the Boy Scouts were allowed to use public grounds when the Fianna boys were not. She worked hard to get a swimming pool opened at Williams Park in Rathmines and battled on for the poor or for those who were too sick, too young or too old to fight for themselves.

The Fianna was taking up much of her time after it was reorganised in 1925 on less military lines and reverted to the *sluagh* system. She was still chief scout. An ambitious programme included classes in the Irish language, archaeology, botany, woodcraft, arts and music, as well as games, physical drill, scouting and first aid. The new Irish Free State government was not prepared to believe that an organisation closely allied with the Volunteers only a few years earlier had given up its militaristic ways. On 3 December 1925, twelve boys who were drilling were arrested in Wexford under the Treasonable Offences Act 1925. One was released and Constance was a witness at the trial of the eleven others two months later.

She reported on the trial for *An Phobhlacht*. When sworn in, she had added to the formal oath, 'I will swear the truth on my allegiance to the Irish Republic'. The judges reprimanded her and asked that she behave with propriety. 'I always behave with propriety, for I am a most proper person, I assure your honour,' she replied, to hoots of appreciation from the Fianna boys in the packed court room.

The defence insisted that the boys were drilling in preparation for a march to the grave of Liam Mellows on 13 December and that if everyone who marched at a funeral procession was accused of military drilling, the jails would be full to overflowing. Not only that, but the Baden Powell scouts drilled in public and could indulge in revolver and musketry practise, while the Fianna forbade the use of firearms. The jury returned a verdict of not guilty.

It was by no means the last time a Fianna boy would be arrested. The Treasonable Offences Act proved an effective weapon in the Free State's fight against republicanism, and the raids, beatings and searches continued. Republicans lucky enough to find work faced possible arrest at any time, which meant they lost their jobs. Thousands were forced to emigrate. With poverty and unemployment rising, a new and more flexible political approach was needed if the fledgling Irish state was to flourish.

That same December, Constance resigned from her position as president of Cumann na mBan after discussions with de Valera about founding a new political party. Because of its abstentionist policy, Sinn Féin had not been able to make its case against the signing of the Boundary Agreement that confirmed the division of Ireland in two. It was time to move on. At the annual convention, Constance withheld her inside knowledge of de Valera's intentions. When a motion condemning any TD who entered the newly formed parliament was passed, Constance was the only dissenter. She announced that she was resigning from her position as Cumann na mBan president since the passing of the resolution would tie her hands 'in the event of certain circumstances arising'.

Without Constance, the Cumann meetings lost some of their sparkle; Sighle Humphreys reported that it nearly broke their hearts to accept her resignation. She was not the ideal chairwoman, drawing caricatures when she was bored and only brightening up when a subject interested her, but she was much loved and respected and an inspirational figure for younger members, especially those who had shared a prison cell with her. A month later, plans to make her a presentation came to nothing on the dubious grounds that she had never been a signed-up member of any Cumann na mBan branch. When elected president in 1916, she was a member of Inghinidhe na hÉireann and had come to Cumann na mBan when Inghinidhe formed a branch of the organisation.

In a letter to Staskou in autumn 1925, Constance admitted that she had been 'very sick' but assured him that her health was now wonderful. She spent most of her spare time driving out to the country and sketching: 'I have been struggling to teach myself water-colours these last few years and am just beginning to express myself in them. Oils were too expensive for me to continue, unless I gave up politics and tried to earn money by them.' She had begun using watercolours when in jail in England where, because she was living in such close quarters with other prisoners, she could could not use oil paints because of their strong smell. An exhibition of forty-one of her paintings from her time in Holloway was well received around this time.

In January, Constance wrote to Staskou again, recommending the novels of Joseph Conrad and telling him that she had cut off her hair. 'I don't see why old women should not be as comfortable as young.' Because there was a fashion for Russian boots, she had fished out the old red boots from Zywotowka and she thought they were the smartest pair in Dublin. Eva, she wrote, was the only real relation she has left. She never saw Josslyn and never wanted to. She did not mention her mother, who had kept in touch with her even through the troubled times by means of assignations at Mespil House, the home of Sarah Purser.

On 8 February 1926, Seán O'Casey's 'immoral' play *The Plough and the Stars* caused riots in the Abbey Theatre. Republicans revealed their latent puritanism by expressing their horror at the sight of a prostitute on stage and an Irish flag in a public house. Even more upsetting was the use of Pearse's words in a manner that was seen as a slur on the men of 1916. Hanna Sheehy Skeffington, Kathleen Clarke and Margaret Pearse were among those protesting, although each had different reasons for their action. Constance stayed away. So bruised was O'Casey by the controversy that he left for London, never to return.

An extraordinary meeting of Sinn Féin was held at Dublin's Rotunda from 9 to 11 March to discuss the future of the party. De Valera argued that, because the government's oppressive policies were going unopposed, the party should take its place in the Dáil and fight those policies; the only remaining stumbling block was the oath. After a furious debate, de Valera's resolution narrowly failed by 223 to 218 votes. De Valera resigned and set about forming a new party to be called Fianna Fáil after the first standing army of Celtic Ireland.

Constance kept herself busy with the new political party, as well as with the Fianna, the Republican Dramatic Society and the Prisoners' Defence League. She continued to speak out against injustice. She supported the State Pension Scheme for Necessitous Mothers. She was closely connected to St Ultan's Infant Hospital, where Kathleen Lynn was vice-chairman and Madeleine ffrench-Mullen secretary. She was tired, but soldiering on. She loved young people and would bring the Coghlan children to Grafton Street, stopping her car outside Woolworth's and making lots of noise, to their great embarrassment. She visited Francis Stuart and Iseult Gonne at their cottage in Glencree. They found her likeable: 'She was warm-hearted, natural, very interested in practical things like how we were living and how we were managing'.

On 16 May 1926, Constance chaired the inaugural meeting of Fianna Fáil, the Soldiers of Destiny, in the La Scala Theatre, off Dublin's O'Connell Street, as Sackville Street was now known. She introduced the main speaker as 'President de Valera'. After the applause had died down, de Valera corrected her, stating 'I am not here as president'. He outlined his plan to get rid of the oath of allegiance and cut the bonds of foreign interference. 'Today we are making a new start for another attempt to get the nation out of the paralysing "Treaty dilemma"', he said. Constitutional methods were to be preferred to physical force; the people of Ireland were tired of bloodshed and conflict.

Writing to Eva around that time, Constance wondered whether 'people get rather mad when they go in for politics'. She gave her opinion on 'the oath', which 'made it absolutely impossible for an honourable person to enter the Free State parliament. De Valera had said he would 'go in' if there was no oath and believed the time had come to demand its removal. She commented that some 'unlogical persons' are howling. These 'self-righteous fools' stood 'for principle and for the honour of the Republic'. How her views had changed!

During this period Constance was unaware that her sister was gravely ill with colon cancer. Eva and Esther had told no one and, in her final eighteen months, Eva devoted herself to writing on religious topics and giving talks to theosophical societies. By January, she was bedridden and Esther's brother Reginald was helping to nurse her.

An office was found on O'Connell Street for the new party, with expenses paid for by friends. Meetings were held all over the country and when the first *ard fheis* was held on 24 November at the Rotunda Buildings in Dublin, more than 500 delegates attended. De Valera was unanimously elected president and Constance was elected to the sixteen-person executive, along with P.J. Routledge and Seán T. O'Kelly (vice-presidents); Seán Lemass and Gerald Boland (honorary secretaries) and Dr James Ryan and Seán McEntee (honorary treasurers). The first executive of Fianna Fáil included six women – Margaret Pearse, Kathleen Clarke, Hanna Sheehy Skeffington, Dorothy Macardle and Linda Kearns, as well as Constance. Apart from Sheehy Skeffington, all would remain staunch members of the party. Writing about the possibility of Constance taking the oath, Eithne Coyle pointed out that 'Madame was no fool ... she had more than average intelligence to realise all the implications involved'.

On 30 June 1926, a month after her fifty-sixth birthday, Eva died; she had taken a turn for the worse two days earlier. Constance, who knew nothing of what was going on, had been away at the seashore for a few days and did not get the telegram with its shattering news until she returned to Frankfort House. She had been depressed for several days, not knowing why until she received the news. 'Everything seemed to go from under me,' she wrote to Esther Roper. Her sister had been her mentor and her guide all their lives. 'She was something wonderful and beautiful, and so simple and thought so little of herself. Her gentleness prevented me getting very callous in a war. I once held out and stopped a man being shot because of her.'

Since her time in Aylesbury Jail, she had developed a habit of imagining her sister's opinion on anything she did. 'Every sketch I made I wondered how she would like it, and I looked forward to showing it to her. If I saw anything beautiful, I thought of her and wished she was there to enjoy it.' In recent times, she had begun her feel her sister's presence again:

> When I'm painting she seems to look at me and help me from the clouds. I wake suddenly and it is just as if she was there. Last

Sunday at Mass, when I wasn't thinking of her at all, she suddenly seemed to smile at me from behind the priest, and I know it is real and that she, the real Eva, is somewhere very near.

She did not go to the funeral, telling a friend that she could not face the family. Mabel and Mordaunt attended but their mother was too ill to travel.

In September, Constance visited Esther Roper in London. She felt her sister's loss deeply but was determined to drive herself on. In the winter of 1926–7, a prolonged coal strike in England meant that Dublin's poor were again starving and freezing. Constance made frequent trips into the Dublin and Wicklow mountains in her old car to collect turf, and she arranged for her friend Lady Albina Broderick, also known as Gobnait Ní Bhrudair, to send turf from Kerry. Men would hold meetings while people froze, she would say. She had come to the belief that meetings were politics as practised by men. She delivered the turf to those who needed it, carrying the heavy bags herself up the dark tenement stairs and then helping to light the fire and tidy up the room.

She continued to charm her admirers: the street traders of Moore Street, the ardent republicans, and a group of hecklers known as 'Madame's Wans'. There was a day out at a holy well in County Meath with the future Fianna Fáil Minister Michael Hilliard, where she sketched for several hours. He remembered her beautiful eyes and distinguished bearing.

In October, the Sinn Féin *ard fheis* attracted only 200 delegates. Women were well represented, or perhaps their presence was more obvious because of the overall drop in numbers. Mary MacSwiney was elected vice-president and Caitlín Brugha became secretary for Dublin. Others elected included Kathleen Lynn, Margaret Buckley, Lily Coventry, Máire Comerford, Dulcibella Barton, Kate O'Callaghan, and Gobnait Ní Bhrudair.

On 11 November 1926, Constance spoke at an anti-Remembrance Day rally along with Maud Gonne MacBride, Charlotte Despard and Tom Kelly. A few weeks later, she unveiled a cross in memory of two Fianna boys, Alf Colley and Seán Cole, captured and killed during the Civil War. She seemed tired.

On 23 January 1927, Constance's mother Georgina died at her home in County Sligo at the age of eighty-five. Constance and her daughter Maeve attended the funeral in Lissadell. She had not seen her brother Josslyn since 1917, although she corresponded with him. She occasionally gave way to sadness at the deaths of her mother and sister. Once a friend entered her room without knocking because she thought Constance had gone out. She found her sitting quietly at the window looking out at the rainy twilight with tears running down her cheeks.

Her last notable outing came at a protest meeting in Rathmines against the government's proposed Electricity Supply Bill in February 1927, where she argued that such a bill would create a state-owned monopoly. In chaotic scenes, and with her dog running around the hall, Constance was ordered by the chairman to sit down. 'I am afraid of no man,' she retorted. 'No one says you are,' was the response. The meeting ended with opposing sides belting out 'God Save the King' and 'The Red Flag'.

In June 1927 came Constance's final general election – the first for the fledgling Fianna Fáil party. The programme included tariffs to promote Irish self-sufficiency, which appealed to Constance. She was fully involved in the campaigning, despite breaking both bones in her lower arm while cranking her beloved car. 'Glory be it's not my jaw, I can still talk,' she said while it was being set. With her arm in a sling, she went on to her meeting and made her speech. However, the broken arm restricted her – she could not paint nor could she drive, and dressing and combing her hair were difficult. In the election, she stood for her old South Dublin City constituency and was elected. The party in power won forty-seven seats – a big drop of sixteen. Fianna Fáil was only three seats behind with forty-four. Sinn Féin had a disaster, winning only five seats – a loss of thirty-nine. Labour took a respectable twenty-two seats, up by eight.

On 23 June, with her arm in a black sling, Constance walked with de Valera to Leinster House to demand admission to the Dáil. She was as tall and imposing as ever, but looked frail. The doors to the chamber inside were locked and they could go no further without taking the despised oath. They returned to their headquarters and addressed a large crowd.

The last in a lifetime of meetings was a gathering of the Fianna Fáil executive in early July. She looked so poorly that one of the young men present suggested she go home but, as he said, 'She was a peculiar woman. She'd sit a meeting out even if she dropped dead.' Still concerned, he surreptitiously asked the chairman to cut the agenda short and took her home to Frankfort House on the tram. Dr Lynn was called and immediately sent her to Sir Patrick Dun's Hospital, where Dr William Taylor, a much-respected medical man, performed an appendectomy. At first she seemed to be recovering. He joked with her about the great streak of antiseptic on her stomach. 'Well, Madame, I never thought I'd see you painted orange.' She responded in kind.

On 7 July, a message broadcast on the radio summoned her family. After a second operation for peritonitis, her condition was critical, though she remained alert and calm. Dorothy Macardle sent a telegram to Josslyn at Lissadell.

She was in a public ward with no privacy and when Éamon de Valera visited; he suggested that she might prefer a private room. He got short shrift. 'She was angry with me because she felt that I was suggesting that what was good enough for the ordinary poor was not good enough for her. She had always helped the worker and the needy and she wanted to be identified with them.' Her daughter Maeve arrived at her bedside as did Esther Roper from London. Along with Helena Molony, Marie Perolz, May Coghlan and Florrie O'Connell, they undertook a vigil on the Saturday, praying for her in the hospital board room.

Constance rallied briefly. Sighle Humphreys came to visit wearing a new pink dress she had bought in Paris, knowing how Constance loved pretty things. In the streets, Esther Roper was stopped by strangers looking for news. 'Ah what would the people in the slums do without her,' said one tearful woman. 'She's given up everything for us and she thinks that what's good enough for us is good enough for her. Please God she'll get better.'

To Constance's great joy, her husband Casimir hurried to Dublin from Warsaw, bringing with him Staskou, the beloved stepson she had not seen for years. She was cheerful and happy. 'This is the happiest day of my life,' she said. When they arrived, Esther Roper was with her. Constance insisted on opening a bunch of roses sent by Josslyn, though her hands were shaking. She did not fear death. 'It is so beautiful to have this love and kindness before I go.' On her last day, she showed May Coghlan how she could lift her tea cup with her right hand. Her broken bone had healed.

Casimir was staying with the Starkeys, artist friends from the old days. At ten o'clock on 14 July, he got a message to come quickly. Constance was drifting away; she spoke of seeing bright lights and said she felt she was being lifted upwards. He was with her when she sank into a coma and, with her face radiant, she died at 1.30am on Friday 15 July. Also at her bedside were Éamon de Valera, Hanna Sheehy Skeffington and May Coghlan. Esther Roper was back in London when she heard the news.

Between the pages of the Catholic bible beside her bed was a typewritten verse 'To Mother and Eva 1927' adapted from Shelley's *Adonais* verses 39 and 40.

They are not dead, they do not sleep;
They have awakened from the dream of life,
They have outsoared the shadow of our night.
Envy and calumny and hate and pain,
And that unrest which men miscall delight,
Can touch them not, nor torture them again.

While ordinary Dubliners mourned one of their champions, both City Hall and the Mansion House, as public properties, were refused for her lying-in-state. She was managing to cause trouble even in death. Instead, her body was taken from St Andrew's Church on Westland Row to the familiar surroundings of the Rotunda, where her casket was guarded by Fianna boys, and long streams passed by to say their final farewell. It was an emotionally charged time in Dublin. Five days before her death, one of her political enemies, Kevin O'Higgins, had been murdered near his home in Booterstown; he was given a full state funeral with children getting the day off school.

Constance's funeral on Sunday, 17 July was one of the biggest ever seen in Dublin. Thousands followed the coffin and thousands more lined the route to Glasnevin Cemetery to say goodbye to their 'Madame'. Leading the procession was her family – Casimir, Stanislaus, Maeve, Sir Josslyn and his wife, Lady Mary Gore-Booth. Eight motor tenders were needed for the wreaths and flowers, sent not only by all the organisations to which she had given such energy, but also by childhood companions, society friends, the rich and the poor of Dublin. Among the donations –

allegedly – were the two dozen eggs one countrywoman had promised she would give Constance when she came out of hospital.

The funeral took two hours to make it through O'Connell Street. Behind the advance guard of Fianna boys came a band, followed by representatives of the Irish Citizen Army, and then another band. More Fianna preceded the coffin wrapped in a tricolour, along with members of the clergy. One of the priests was Father Tom Ryan, chaplain at Kilmainham in 1916 when Constance had asked him to be with her at the end, thinking it would be then. He kept his promise to her eleven years later. Fianna Fáil and Republican deputies followed, with more bands, several contingents of Volunteers, members of the Workers' Union, Cumann na mBan, Clan na nGaedheal, and the Women's Defence League, led by Maud Gonne MacBride and Charlotte Despard. Mary MacSwiney and J.J. O'Kelly led the Sinn Féin representatives.

In the crowd were members of the old Citizen Army, mothers from the poorer parts of Dublin, and thousands more whose lives had been touched by a big-hearted, generous and brave woman, whose essential humanity had sometimes found her at odds with the harsh and often brutal reality of Irish politics. At three o'clock, when the advance guard reached Glasnevin, one hundred Free State soldiers with rifles had taken up position a short distance from her grave, while a number of detectives mingled with the crowd. At the chapel, the rosary was recited in Irish and the coffin taken to the vault.

Éamon de Valera gave the oration:

> Madame Markievicz is gone from us, Madame, the friend of the toiler, the lover of the poor. Ease and station she put aside, and took the hard way of service with the weak and the down-trodden. Sacrifice, misunderstanding and scorn lay on the road she adopted, but she trod it unflinchingly.

He applauded

> this wonderful outcrop of Irish landlordism and Dublin Castle, this brilliant, fascinating, incomprehensible rebel ... consumed with the fires of a burning devotion to whatever cause happened to capture her restless and enthusiastic, intellectual personality.

She now lies at rest with her fellow champions of the right – mourned by the people whose liberties she fought for; blessed by the loving prayers of the poor she tried so hard to befriend. The world knew her only as a soldier of Ireland, but we knew her as a colleague and comrade.

We knew the kindliness, the great woman's heart of her, the great Irish soul of her, and we know the loss we have suffered is not to be repaired. It is sadly we take our leave, but we pray high heaven that all she longed for may one day be achieved.

The burial was postponed because gravediggers did not work on Sundays. A day later, Constance was laid to rest, watched by Free State military, uniformed police and detectives. They had remained on duty at the cemetery all day. The last post was sounded by buglers of Fianna Éireann and the uniform Constance wore at the Royal College of Surgeons in 1916 was lowered into the grave with her. For weeks after, the family received letters of condolence from public bodies, those who had worked with her and many ordinary people who had loved and admired her, even those who felt that her life had followed an unfortunate path.

On 11 August 1927, having signed the Oath of Allegiance in front of a representative of the governor general of the Irish Free State, the Fianna Fáil TDs entered the Dáil. De Valera took the Oath while claiming that he was simply signing a slip of paper to gain a right of participation in the Dáil. An election was called on 15 September; Cumann na nGaedheal was returned to power but with a reduced majority. Sinn Féin, clinging to the fantasy that the surviving members of the Second Dáil constituted the legitimate government of Ireland, opted not to contest the election, distancing itself from the political mainstream for decades to come.

After ten years of Cumann na nGaedheal, which had brought the country bloodshed, repression, unemployment, a drop in pensions and public pay, and a reduced role for women in public life, Fianna Fáil came to power in 1932. In the years following, xenophobia, economic protectionism and an authoritarian government helped ensure that women's rights were further eroded. Those with a wider vision emigrated. The Oireachtas enacted a marriage bar for civil servants, including widows; it brought in lower pay rates for women teachers and made jury service non-compulsory for women, which meant that women who had the misfortune to fall foul of the law would be judged by all-male juries. There was a ban on contraceptives, strictly no divorce, and a limit on female employment in industry. Women's primary role as 'housewives and mothers' was enshrined in de Valera's 1937 Constitution. Feminists found little support in a world where women, wearied by war, returned to a more traditional way of life, and regarded any foreign influence with suspicion, especially in matters of morality. All over Europe, the gains made by strong, brave women like Constance Markievicz were eradicated.

Romantic Ireland was – emphatically – dead and gone.

Sources and Bibliography

By Constance Markievicz

Diary 1892–93 (National Museum, Collins Barracks).

Prison Letters of Countess Markievicz, ed. Esther Roper (London: Virago Press, 1987).

What Irish Republicans Stand For (Glasgow: Civic Press, 1922).

James Connolly's Policy and Catholic Doctrine (1924).

Free Women in a Free Nation (*Bean na hÉireann*, February 1909).

The Women of '98 (*Irish Citizen*, 6, 13, 20, 27 November and 4 December 1915).

A Call to the Women of Ireland (Dublin, Fergus O'Connor, 1918).

Break Down the Bastilles (*Voice of Labour*, 1 May 1919).

On the Run, undated, hand written article.

The Police, 16 December 1919, handwritten article.

Peace with Honour (*Phoblacht na hÉireann*, 3 January 1922).

Women in the Fight, Roger McHugh (ed.) Dublin 1916 (1966).

Conditions of Women in English Jails (*New Ireland*, 8 and 15 October 1922).

Tom Clarke and the first Day of the Republic (*Éire*, 26 May 1923).

Na Fianna (*Éire*, 9 June 1923).

Larkin, the Fianna and the King's Visit (*Éire*, 16 June 1923).

Memories of the King's Visit, 1911 (*Éire*, 14, 21, 28 July; 4 August 1923).

Mr. Arthur Griffith and the Sinn Féin Organisation (*Éire*, 18 and 25 August 1923).

Fianna Éireann and the 1921 Treaty (*Sinn Féin*, 21 June 1924).

Wolfe Tone's Ideals of Democracy (*An Phoblacht*, 26 June 1925).

How We Won the Fianna Trials (*An Phoblacht*, 5 March 1926).

Liam Mellows (*An Phoblacht*, 28 May 1926).

James Connolly as I Knew Him (*The Nation*, 26 March 1927).

1916 (*The Nation*, 23 April 1927).

Citizenship (*Éire*, 13 August 1927).

Blood Money: A One-Act Play (1925).

The Invincible Mother: A One-Act Play (1925).

Broken Dreams: A Three-Act Play (1927).

Books

Andrews, C.S., *Dublin Made Me* (Dublin: Mercier Press, 1979).

Arrington, Laurie, *Revolutionary Lives – Constance and Casimir Markievicz* (New Jersey: Princeton University Press, 2016).

Barton, Brian, *The Secret Court Martial Records of the Easter Rising* (Stroud: The History Press, 2010).

Bowen, Elizabeth, *The Shelbourne* (London: George G Harrap, 1951).

Boylan, Patricia, *All Cultivated People: A History of the United Arts Club Dublin* (London: Colin Smythe, 1988).

Brennan, Robert, Allegiance (Dublin: Brown and Nolan, 1950)

Breen, Timothy Murphy, *The Government's Executions Policy during the Irish Civil War 1922–1923* (NUI, Maynooth, PhD thesis, 2010).

Clarke, Kathleen, *Revolutionary Woman: An Autobiography 1878–1972* (Dublin: O'Brien Press, 2008).

Clare, Anne, *Unlikely Rebels: The Gifford Girls and the Fight for Irish Freedom* (Cork: Mercier Press, 2011).

Coldrey, Barry M, *Faith and Fatherland – the Christian Brothers and the Development of Irish Nationalism 1838–1921* (Dublin: Gill and Macmillan, 1988)

Colum, Mary, *Life and the Dream* (London: Macmillan, 1947)

Connell, Joseph E.A., *Dublin in Rebellion: A directory 1913–1923* (Dublin: The Lilliput Press, 2009).

Connolly, James, *The Re-Conquest of Ireland* (Dublin: New Book Publications, 1972).

—, *Labour in Irish History* (Dublin: New Book Publications, 1971).

—, *Labour, Nationality and Religion* (Dublin: New Book Publications, 1969).

—, *Selected Writings* (ed. P. Beresford Ellis) (London: Pelican, 1975).

Connolly-O'Brien, Nora, *Portrait of a Rebel Father* (Dublin: Four Masters, 1975).

Coogan, Tim Pat, *De Valera: Long Fellow, Long Shadow* (London: Hutchinson, 1993).

Coxhead, Erin, *Daughters of Erin* (London: Colin Smythe, 1979).

Cullen, Clara (ed.), *The World Upturning: Elsie Henry's Irish Wartime Diaries 1913–1919* (Dublin: Merrion Press, 2013).

Cullen Owens, Rosemary, *Louie Bennett* (Cork: Cork University Press, 2001).

Curry, James, *Artist of the Revolution: The Cartoons of Ernest Kavanagh* (Cork: Mercier Press, 2012).

Czira, Sidney Gifford, *The Years Flew By* (Dublin: Gifford and Craven, 1974).

Dangerfield, George, *The Damnable Question: A Study in Anglo-Irish Relations* (London: Constable, 1977).

Davis, Graham (ed.), *In Search of a Better Life: British and Irish Migration* (Stroud: The History Press, 2011).

Dickinson, P.L., *Dublin of Yesteryear* (London: Methuen, 1929)

Dooley, Chris, *Redmond: A Life Undone* (Dublin: Gill and Macmillan, 2015).

Fanning, Ronan, *Fatal Path: British Government and Irish Revolutions 1910–1922* (London: Faber and Faber, 2013).

—, *Eamon de Valera: A Will to Power* (London: Faber and Faber, 2015)

Feeney, Brian, *16 Lives: Seán Mac Diarmada* (Dublin: O'Brien Press, 2014).

Ferriter, Diarmaid, *The Transformation of Ireland 1900–2000* (London: Profile Press, 2004).

—, *Judging Dev* (Dublin: Royal Irish Academy, 2007).

—, *A Nation and not a Rabble: The Irish Revolution 1913–1923* (London: Profile Books, 2015).

Figgis, Darrell, *AE (George W. Russell)* (New York: Dodd, Mead and Company, 1916).

Fingall, Elizabeth, Countess of, *Seventy Years Young* (Dublin: The Lilliput Press, 1991).

Fitz-Simons, Christopher, *Eleven Houses* (London: Penguin Ireland, 2007).

Forester, Margery, *Michael Collins, Lost Leader* (London: Sphere Books, 1972).

Foster, R.F., *Vivid Faces – The Revolutionary Generation in Ireland 1890–1923* (London: Allen Lane, 2014).

—, *Modern Ireland 1600–1972* (London: Penguin, 1989).

—, *W.B. Yeats: A Life, Vol 1: The Apprentice Mage 1865–1914* (Oxford: University Press, 1997).

—, *W.B. Yeats: A Life, Vol 2: The Arch-Poet 1915–1939* (Oxford: University Press, 2003).

Foy, Michael T. and Barton, Brian, *The Easter Rising* (Stroud: The History Press, 2011).

Fox, R.M., *Rebel Irishwomen* (Dublin and Cork: The Talbot Press, 1935).

—, *The History of the Irish Citizen Army* (Dublin: J. Duffy, 1944).

Gaughan, J. Anthony, *Scouting in Ireland* (Dublin: Kingdom Books, 2006).

—, *The Memories of Constable Jeremiah Mee RIC* (Cork: Mercier Press, 2012).

Gore-Booth, Eva, *Death of Fionavar* (London: Erskine Macdonald, 1916).

Gregory, Augusta, Lady, *Lady Gregory's Journals 1916–1930*, ed. Lennox Robinson (London: Putnam and Company, 1946).

Haverty, Anne, *Constance Markievicz: An Independent Life* (London: Pandora, 1993).

Hay, Marnie, *Bulmer Hobson and the Nationalist Movement in Twentieth-Century Ireland* (Manchester: Manchester University Press, 2009).

Hobson, Bulmer, *A Short History of the Irish Volunteers* (Dublin: The Candle Press, 1918).

Hughes, Brian, *16 Lives: Michael Mallin* (Dublin: O'Brien Press, 2012).

James, Dermot, *The Gore-Booths of Lissadell* (Dublin: Woodfield Press, 2004).

Keohane, Leo, *Captain Jack White, Imperialism, Anarchism and the Irish Citizen Army* (Dublin: Merrion Press, 2014).

Knirck, Jason, *Women of the Dáil* (Dublin: Irish Academic Press, 2006).

Lee, J.J, *Ireland 1912–1986: Politics and Society* (Cambridge: Cambridge University Press, 1993).

Lyons, F.S.L., *Ireland since the Famine* (London: Fontana, 1986).

MacBride, Maud Gonne, *A Servant of the Queen* (London: Victor Gollancz, 1992).

Marreco, Anne, *The Rebel Countess: The Life and Times of Constance Markievicz* (London: Phoenix Press, 1967).

Martin, F.X. (ed.), *The Irish Volunteers 1913–1915: Recollections and Documents* (Dublin: Merrion Press, 2013).

— (ed.), *The Howth Gun Running and the Kilcoole Gun Running: Recollections and Documents* (Dublin: Merrion Press, 2014).

— (ed.), *Leaders and Men of the Easter Rising: Dublin 1916* (London: Methuen, 1967).

Martin, F.X. and F. J. Byrne (eds), *The Scholar Revolutionary: Eoin MacNeill 1867–1945 and the Making of the New Ireland* (Shannon: Irish University Press, 1973).

Matthews, Anne, *Renegades – Irish Republican Women 1900–1922* (Cork: Mercier Press, 2010).

—, *Dissidents - Irish Republican Women 1923–1941* (Cork: Mercier Press, 2012).

—, *The Irish Citizen Army* (Cork: Mercier Press, 2014).

McCarthy, Cal, *Cumann na mBan and the Irish Revolution* (Cork: Collins Press, 2007).

McConville, Michael, *Ascendancy to Oblivion: The Story of the Anglo Irish* (London: Quartet, 1986).

McConville, Seán, *Irish Political Prisoners 1848–1922* (London: Routledge, 2003).

McCoole, Sinead, *No Ordinary Women: Irish Female Activists in the Revolutionary Years 1900–1923* (Dublin: O'Brien Press, 2008).

—, *Easter Widows* (London: Doubleday Ireland, 2014).

McGowan, Joe (ed.), *Constance Markievicz: The People's Countess* (Sligo: Constance Markievicz Millennium Committee, 2003).

Mitchell, Arthur, *Revolutionary Government in Ireland: Dáil Éireann 1919–1921* (Dublin: Gill and Macmillan, 1993).

Nevin, Donal, *James Connolly: A Full Life* (Dublin: Gill and Macmillan, 2005).

— (ed.), *James Larkin Lion of the Fold* (Dublin: Gill and Macmillan, 2006).

Nic Shuibhlaigh, Máire, *The Splendid Years* (Dublin: Duffy, 1955).

Norman, Diana, *Terrible Beauty: A Life of Constance Markievicz, 1868–1927* (Swords: Poolbeg Press, 1987).

O'Brien, Paul, *1916 in Focus: Shootout: The Battle for St Stephen's Green 1916* (Dublin: New Island, 2013).

O'Casey, Seán, *The Story of the Irish Citizen Army, 1913–1916* (Libcom.org/library/story-irish-citizen-army-sean-ocasey).

—, *Three Dublin Plays* (London: Faber and Faber, 1988).

—, *Autobiography Volume 3: Drums Under the Windows* (London: Pan Books, 1972).

O'Connor, Emmett, *A Labour History of Ireland 1824–2000* (Dublin: UCD Press, 2011).

O'Faolain, Nuala, *The Story of Chicago May* (London: Michael Joseph, 2005).

O'Faolain, Seán, *Constance Markievicz* (London: Cresset Library, 1987).

—, *The Irish* (London: Pelican, 1969).

Ó hÓgartaigh, Margaret, *Kathleen Lynn: Irishwoman, Patriot, Doctor* (Dublin: Irish Academic Press, 2006).

Oikarinin, Sari, *A Dream of Liberty: Constance Markievicz's Vision of Ireland 1908–1927* (Helsinki: Suomen Historiallinem Seura, 1998).

O'Neill, Marie, *From Parnell to de Valera – a Biography of Jennie Wyse Power* (Dublin: Blackwater Press, 1991).

O'Rahilly, Aodogán, *The O'Rahilly: A Secret History of the Rebellion of 1916* (Dublin: The Lilliput Press, 1991 and 2016).

Pearse, Patrick, *The Coming Revolution: The Political Writings and Speeches of Patrick Pearse* (Cork: Mercier, 2012).

Pešeta, Sonia, *Irish Nationalist Women 1900–1918* (Cambridge: Cambridge University Press, 2013).

Plunkett Dillon, Geraldine, *All in the Blood* (ed. Honor Ó Brolchain) (Dublin: A & A Farmar, 2006).

Quigley, Patrick, *The Polish Irishman – the Life and Times of Count Casimir Markievicz* (Dublin: Liffey Press, 2012).

Quinlan, Carmel, *Genteel Revolutionaries: Anna and Thomas Haslam and the Irish Women's Movement* (Cork: Cork University Press, 2005).

Ryan, Desmond, *Remembering Sion* (London: Arthur Baker, 1934) Desmond

—, *The Rising* (Dublin: Golden Eagle, 1957)

Ryan, Louise and Ward, Margaret (eds), *Irish Women and the Vote: Becoming Citizens* (Dublin: Irish Academic Press, 2007).

Scourer, Clive, *Maeve de Markievicz – Daughter of Constance* (Killyleagh, Co Down: Clive Scourer, 2003)

Skinnider, Margaret, *Doing My Bit for Ireland* (New York: The Century Company, 1917).

Smith, Nadia Clare, *Dorothy Macardle – A Life* (Dublin: Woodfield Press, 2007)

Stephens, James, *The Insurrection in Dublin* (MacMillan: New York, 1917).

Tiernan, Sonja, *Eva Gore-Booth – an Image of Such Politics* (Manchester: Manchester University Press, 2012).

— (ed.), *The Political Writings of Eva Gore Booth* (Manchester: Manchester University Press, 2015).

Torchiana, Donald T., *W.B. Yeats and Georgian Ireland* (Evanston, Illinois: Northwestern University Press, 1966).

Townshend, Charles, *Easter 1916* (London: Allen Lane, 2005).

—, *The Republic* (London: Allen Lane, 2013).

Van Voris, Jacqueline, *Constance de Markievicz in the Cause of Ireland* (Amherst: University of Massachusetts Press, 1967).

Walsh, Maurice, *Bitter Freedom – Ireland in a Revolutioanry World 1918–1923* (London: Faber and Faber, 2015).

—, *The News from Ireland* (London: I.B. Tauris, 2008).

Ward, Margaret, *Maud Gonne: Ireland's Joan of Arc* (London: Pandora, 1990).

—, *Unmanageable Revolutionaries* (London: Pluto Press, 1995).

—, *Hanna Sheehy Skeffington: A Life* (Cork: Attic Press, 1997).

— (ed.), *In Their Own Voices: Women and Irish Nationalism* (Cork: Attic Press, 2001).

Wheeler, Charles Newton, *The Irish Republic* (Chicago: Cahill-Igoe Company, 1919).

Yeates, Padraig, *Lock-Out: Dublin 1913* (Dublin: Gill and Macmillan, 2000).

Yeats, W.B., *Selected Poetry* (ed. A. Norman Jeffares) (London: Papermac, 1971).

—, *The Autobiography* (New York: Collier Books, 1965).

—, *The Collected Letters* Vols, 1, 2, 3 (general ed. John Kelly) (Oxford: Clarendon Press, 1997).

Articles

Farrell, Brian, 'Markievicz and the women of the revolution' in F.X. Martin (ed.), *Leaders and Men of the Easter Rising: Dublin 1916* (London: Methuen, 1967).

Hay, Marnie, 'The Foundation and Development of Na Fianna Éireann, 1909–16 ', *Irish Historical Studies*, May 2008.

O Briain, Liam, 'Saint Stephen's Green Area', *Capuchin Annual*, 1966.

Rooney, Philip, 'The Green Jacket – the Story of the Countess' (serialised *Sunday Press*, Dublin, 11 September to 30 October 1960).

Sheehy Skeffington, Hanna, 'British Militarism as I Have Known It', Tralee: *Kerryman*, 1946.

—, 'Constance Markievicz and What She Stood for', *An Phoblacht*, 16 July 1932, pp. 7–8.

—, 'Reminiscences of an Irish Suffragette', *The Field Day Anthology of Irish Writing*, Vols IV/V (Cork University Press, 1991; ed. Angela Bourke).

Other Sources

Royal Commission on the Rebellion in Ireland (London, 1916).

The Peace Treaty with Germany

Dáil Reports, 1918–1925.

Newspapers and Periodicals

Bean na hÉireann

Capuchin Annual 1966

The Fenian

Freeman's Journal

History Ireland

Irish Citizen

Irish Independent

Irish Times

Irish Worker

The Nation

An Phoblacht

Sinn Féin

Sligo Champion

Sunday Press

The Times

Bureau of Military History Witness Statements

St Stephen's Green:

WS 258 Maeve Cavanagh

WS 256 Nellie Donnelly

WS 382, Thomas Mallin

WS 505 Seán Moylan

WS 907 Laurence Nugent

WS 296 Harry Nicholls

WS 6 Liam Ó Briain

WS 1766 William O'Brien

WS1666 Thomas O'Donoghue

WS 421 William Oman

WS 733 James O'Shea

WS 585 Frank Robbins

WS 246 Marie Perolz

Other

WS 483 Maurice Aherne

WS 645 Nora Ashe

WS 251 Richard Balfe

WS 723 Alice Barry

WS 1754 Leslie Bean Ui Barry (Leslie Price)

WS 936 Dulcibella Barton

WS 979 Robert C. Barton

WS 385 Mrs Seán Beaumont (Maureen McGavock)

WS 939 Ernest Blythe

WS 779 Robert Brennan

WS 1,019 Alfred Bucknill

WS 58 Seamus Cashin

WS 258 Maeve Cavanagh (Mrs Mac Donnell)

WS 266 Áine Ceannt

WS 919 Ina Connolly-Heron

WS 1,349 Daniel Conway

WS 179 Elizabeth and Nell Corr

WS 750 Eithne Coyle

WS 909 Sidney Czira

WS 327 Patrick Egan

WS 216 Louise Gavan Duffy

WS 700 St John Gogarty

WS 546 Rose Hackett

WS 76 John Hanratty

WS 30, 31, 51 Bulmer Hobson

WS 280 Robert Holland

WS 328 Garry Holohan

WS 217 John J. Keegan

WS 842 Seán Kennedy

WS 494 Peter Kiernan

WS 357 Kathleen Lynn

WS 317 Maud Gonne MacBride

WS 219 John MacDonagh

WS 1,377 Hugo (Aodh) MacNeill

WS 382 Thomas Mann

WS 100 Patrick McCartan

WS 1,497 Joseph McCarthy

WS 290 Seán McLoughlin

WS 306 Michael McDunphy

WS 1,013 P.J. McElligott

WS 244 John McGallogly

WS 379 Jeremiah Mee

WS 391 Helena Molony

WS 11080 Patrick Mullolly

WS 296 Harry Nicholls

WS 1,369 James Nolan

WS 323 Liam O'Brien

WS 1766 William O'Brien

WS 321 Máire Ó Brolchain

WS 1,666 Father Thomas O'Donoghue

WS 193 Senator Seamus O'Farrell

WS 1235 William O'Flynn

WS 161 Donal O'Hannigan

WS 5841 Patrick Sarsfield O'Hegarty

WS 384 J.J. O'Kelly ("Sceilg")

WS 180 Kathleen O'Kelly

WS 1,108 Jeremiah J. (Diarmuid) O'Leary

WS 1,219 Seán O'Neill

WS 1728 Nioclas O Nuallain

WS 333 Áine O'Rahilly

WS 246 Marie Perolz

WS 257 Grace Plunkett

WS 267 Seamus Pounch

WS 191 Joseph Reynolds

WS 817 Seán Saunders

WS 288 Lieutenant Colonel Charles Saurin

WS 892 Very Reverend T.J. Shanley

WS 334 Eugene Smith

WS 0230 John Southwell

WS 139 Michael Walker

WS 1,140 Patrick Ward

WS 1420 Patrick Whelan

WS 1,207 Alfred White (Ailfred de Faoite)

Public Records Office of Northern Ireland

Lissadell Papers

National Library of Ireland

Constance Markievicz papers

Joseph McGarrity papers

Hanna Sheehy Skeffington papers

Public Records Office, London

Sinn Féin and Republican Suspects 1899–1921: Dublin Special Branch Files CO 904 (193–216)

Home Office, Activities of Countess Markievicz 1916–1920 HO 144/1580/316818

War Office: Army of Ireland: Administrative and Easter Rising Records 1 June 1918-30 June 1919 WO 35/210

Websites

www.theirishrevolution.wordpress.com

www.garda.ie

www.bureauofmilitaryhistory.ie

www.warofindependence.info

www.firstworldwar.com

www.fiannaeireannhistory.wordpress.com

Index